Wilbur Wilson Thoburn

In terms of life

sermons and talks to college students

Wilbur Wilson Thoburn

In terms of life
sermons and talks to college students

ISBN/EAN: 9783744744942

Printed in Europe, USA, Canada, Australia, Japan

Cover: Foto ©Lupo / pixelio.de

More available books at **www.hansebooks.com**

W. W. Thoburn.

IN TERMS OF LIFE

SERMONS AND TALKS
TO COLLEGE STUDENTS

BY

WILBUR W. THOBURN

LATE PROFESSOR OF BIONOMICS
IN THE LELAND STANFORD JUNIOR UNIVERSITY

17032

STANFORD UNIVERSITY, CALIFORNIA

PUBLISHED BY THE UNIVERSITY

1899

The Murdock Press, San Francisco

CONTENTS.

PREFATORY.

In one of his lecture talks, included in this volume, Dr. Thoburn deprecates the very natural desire of certain students to possess his printed words. With him this was more than a passing feeling. He believed in the living message, and he aimed, as all good teachers do, at stirring the activities rather than storing the mind. The emphasis put upon this point must bear some of the blame that so little of all he said was written down. Yet he did look forward to the possibility of some time putting into print the things he was struggling to formulate. And as his thought ripened he seems to have felt more and more the impulse to commit himself to manuscript. To the last, however, the use of manuscript in pulpit or lecture-room was hampering, and even with his most finished work the inspiration of the occasion often led him in delivery to far overleap the written

7

bounds. This was particularly true of his
lectures, which he had never set himself to
write out in full.

The sermons here included are all, with
the exception of the unnamed fragment,
substantially complete. The sermon on
Liberty, the first one given in the University Chapel, is the only one not prepared
specifically for the University. Its quality,
however, is not different from all the rest.
It should be noted that many of the lecture
fragments are also sermon fragments. Those
on Rest and Immortality are not very different from the sermons as actually delivered;
that on Prayer is the basis of his sermon
on the same subject.

Of the lecture fragments not one is complete. Several are hardly more than outline
fragments, included here because of some
characteristic tone not presented so strikingly
elsewhere. Religion as a Social Factor, as
here written, forms about half of his first
lecture at the Coronado Summer School of
1896. The others are mainly special topics
in his course on the Life and Teachings of

Christ, the full lectures existing merely in outline.

It is hardly necessary to add that nothing here included had been made ready for publication. To have done this would have required, from Dr. Thoburn's point of view, a severe revision, much amplification, and of course the elimination of repetitions. What is here fragmentary would have been rounded out to something like completeness. Some statements — graspings at truth — would doubtless have been modified: he himself felt often that he had failed in his formulation, and that he should reach a more adequate and satisfactory expression. But, after all, that book would not have been different from this — only a larger and riper interpretation of a life singularly sweet and wholesome. It is his life in these fragments that will live. To his old students and friends they will bring back the unassuming, helpful presence, the resonant moral atmosphere in which he lived and worked; and to college students who have never known his presence, but who face the same problems, it does not

seem too much to believe that these printed
words will come with something of the same
illuminating and healing ministration. There
is nothing here that can hurt; there is no
wanton or unloving touch; all is helpful and
hopeful and onward.

It only remains to note the possibility of
misquotations, and that in some cases quota-
tion-marks may have been misplaced or
omitted altogether. These and doubtless
other errors have been rendered unavoidable
by the hasty and temporary character of the
manuscript.

O. L. E.

June, 1899.

I.— SERMONS

Our Father — Father of our Lord and Master, and our Father. Who shall measure the depth of the riches both of the wisdom and the knowledge of God! How unsearchable are his judgments, and his ways past tracing out! For who hath known thy mind, O Lord? or who hath been thy counsellor? or who hath first given to thee, and it shall be recompensed unto him again? For of thee and through thee and unto thee are all things. Yet thou art our Father, and for this cause we bow our knees unto thee, of whom all men are named, that thou wouldst grant us, according to the riches of thy glory, that we may be strengthened with power through thy spirit in the inward man: that Christ may dwell in our hearts by faith; to the end that we, being rooted and grounded in love, may be strong to apprehend with all the good what is the

13

*breadth and length and height and depth,
and to know the love of Christ which
passeth knowledge, that we may be filled
with all the fullness of God.*

*May thy kingdom come and thy will be
done.   Give us from day to day food for
our needs.   Forsake us not in our trials.
Guard us from all evil.   Forgive our trans-
gressions.   Help us to be forgiving.   And
unto thee, who art able to do exceeding
abundantly, above all that we can ask or
think, according as the power for receiving worketh in us, to thee be glory, for
ever.   Amen.*

THE WAY

1703 2

" I am the Way." Christ is speaking
— speaking of himself. A quick way to
know a man is to watch him when he is
speaking about himself. Some cannot
speak respectfully of themselves. They
deserve no respect. Others talk to their
own ears about themselves. They are
egotists. Others talk *themselves* to those
who have ears to hear. Listen to these;
they are like children, and deal with the
truth.

Christ often speaks of himself. I
know of no other religious teacher who
does so much of it. And yet one always
feels that his thoughts are not with himself, but with those to whom he is giving
himself helpfully. No one could call
Christ an egotist. There are teachers
who have wonderful power in selecting
beautiful thoughts and pictures out of
the records of the past, and passing them

on to others. They have an instinct for ideals, and they build Utopias of them that make this dusty world seem uncomfortable, and their intoxicated followers never get a sober view of life without turning pessimists.

Again, there are teachers who talk about life and what they get out of it, who exhibit the handful of nuggets they have dug and tell where they found them. And as we listen we are aroused to dig, too. Their hopeful and successful lives quicken ours. Christ belonged to this second class. There is a peculiar power in his "I say unto you." One feels that he has lived his words and that they can be lived. Solomon holds up ideals and precepts, but does not live them. And every view of Solomon we get through his words shows a pessimist whom life has soured. We feel like saying, "Solomon, take your own medicine,"— "Physician, heal thyself." The ideal of Christ is himself, and because he was so much of a man and dealt so much with commonplace things, we feel that we can do as he did.

Precepts and rules of life and high ideals are useful as they mold and shape us while we behold them. They are food for action. They are not guides to life. Habits are guides to living, and habits are formed by doing. One cannot stop at every cross-road to consult a note-book for the proper precept.

Men are neither trained nor saved by being preached at. They seem to enjoy it, and often pay liberally for a weekly exhibition of beautiful ideals and well-worded proverbs. These delight and amuse them as the bottles on the druggist's shelves amuse a child,— but they make wry faces if asked to taste them.

A patriarch, a preacher, who is surrounded by a family of men and women, said: "I never tried to talk religion to my children but once. I got my little girl, one Sunday afternoon, and preached at her. Next week I said, 'Come, let papa talk to you.' She said, 'All right, papa; but please do not talk as you did last Sunday.'"

Far more reaching than a father's words — and fathers are apt to be popes

in their families — is a father's life; and
a mother is not a collection of fine sayings, but an eternal influence of finer
acts.   I have heard more than one mother
mourn because she could not *say* the right
thing, who was all the time an incarnation, in her world of boys and girls, of
the living God. Men and women are
molded by the silent, constant influence
of a home far more than by the daily
scolding and advising. Morning prayers
are a poor substitute for a day of religion.   A home saturated with peace and
purity is the larger part of the training
of every child.   Schools and universities
are extras to be added later.

In the old days a father built a home
for his family.   It was complete in every
part, but the altar around which they
gathered in prayer had yet no place.
The mother wished it in the kitchen.
There she was perplexed with her many
cares. The father wished it in his study.
God seemed nearer to him among his
books. The son wished it in the room
where guests were received, that the stranger entering might know they worshiped

God. So they agreed to leave the matter to
the youngest, who was a little child. Now,
the altar was a shaft of polished wood,
very fragrant, and the child, who loved
most of all to sit before the great fire
and see beautiful forms in the flames,
said, "See, the log is gone; put it there."
So because one would not yield to the
other, they obeyed, and the log was con-
sumed, and its sweet odors filled the
whole house — the kitchen, the study, and
the guest-hall,—and the child saw beautiful forms in the flames.

We can never define or limit our influence upon men and women by words.
Good or bad, it will always vary with
the amount of ourselves we put into our
words. Far more important than anything you learn here, than any phrases
or precepts you hear, is the use you
make of them.

You will be deceived, chiefly by your-
selves. These early college days are a
springtime with you, and the early shoots
of spring are larger and weaker than the
later summer growths. You will think
you are learning far more than you are

learning. The screaming eagle on the
silver does not make it worth a dollar,
though it may pass for one. After years
of talking and acting, of appearing to be,
of trying and failing and succeeding, you
will be valued at your true worth. There
is a premium on truthfulness; and the
more of ourselves we can express in our
living, so much more will we be useful
to our fellows. Personality counts. It
is our intrinsic worth. A bubble may
be a thousand times as large as a pellet
of lead, and far more showy, yet on
the scales the lead weighs down many
bubbles. Gravitation is never deceived
by appearances. The tests of life are
as minute and searching. At the end
of threescore and ten years of living
a man will be known very much as he
knows himself. His value as a social
factor will be measured by the force he
can put into the personal pronoun that
expresses his being. No one who is true
need be afraid of saying, "I say unto
you." I saw this room crowded nearly
from floor to ceiling to hear Mrs. Booth.
I have seen many crowds here, but never

one so moved as when that little woman talked of that for which she stood. No acting could equal it. She was her own credentials. No one else could have done it. Her life of truth and devotion was being vocalized, and those who cared little for the Salvation Army were overwhelmed by the truth incarnated. It is always so. It is this element in Christ's teaching that gives it power. He spoke himself. He was the truth. If he had not been true, men would have known it. We can lie with our lips, but not with our lives. Christ was not killed because he was false, but because other men did not like the contrast between his life and theirs.

Any comparison of Christ with other religious teachers must notice this peculiarity: without exception they stand and point the way; they talk about the truth. Christ says, I am the way, follow *me*: I am the truth, believe *me*. Other teachers talk about God and his attributes and how to reach him, but when Philip asks Christ to show him the Father, he points to himself and says, "Have I been so

long time with you and yet hast thou
not known me, Philip?"—"He that hath
seen me [that is, a true man] hath seen
all of God that human eyes ever can
see." Whatever definition of God men
may crave to satisfy their philosophical
instincts, Christ's conception of God is
the only one that men can live with.
Men have been led far afield by doctrines
about God; but when burdens are heavy
and the men are tired, when life is real
and nothing but the home-feeling can satisfy, then they turn from definitions to
Christ's God and rest in the presence of
the Father. Reason may laugh at it and
call it man-worship, and talk about abstract and unlivable deity. But if it is a
weakness, it is one that strong men often
cultivate. The God incarnated in the
race is the God of Christ, the humanized
God of our daily experience. He brings
back to people the absentee deity which
philosophy is forever moving from one
corner of the universe to another, and puts
him once more in human hearts and says
to men, "There is your God; worship
him — where and how you please,—but

if you want him to stay with you, you must stay with him and lead his life and busy yourself with his business."

Within, you have the raw material to make your Father's image, but you can take the same stuff and make many worse things of it. Christ saw this truth, and pointing to himself as a son of man, living his best, *true*, he said, "He that hath seen me hath seen the Father." And any one of us may do the same. We may point to that in us which is good and true and say, "This is the Father." I hope to grow more and more of him within me until I am full of him, an incarnation.

Now, please do not commence to analyze these words and distribute them among your theological pigeonholes to see what kind of an *arian* I am, or what manner of *ism* this is. Try it by the test of life, and if it works, it is of God and true. It will reveal you to yourself. It will glorify your life. It will help you to conquer yourself. It will show you God in an expanding revelation around and within you, increasing his influence as you increase your touch with him, reacting upon you as you act with him, making your goodness the product of *the* goodness, your truth a fragment of all truth, your life eternal life.

A man can know that he is a son of God only as he feels it in himself, only as he sees, just as any growing boy comes to see, that he and his father are made of the same stuff and by the same pattern. When a man learns this truth he is a made man. When he sees that his affairs and God's are one, when the things he wants to do are the things he sees God wants done, when his Father's business is his business, then he is saved. It is a good word, lightly and flippantly used sometimes, but we can load it full of meaning,— saved from wastefulness, from anxiety about things that last only a little while, saved to live with eternal things forever.

But a man is very lonely when he lives apart from God. When he looks upon the great world-movements as a student only, from the outside, he makes an outcast and an alien of himself. When his

world and *the* world are separate,— himself and his God two beings with distinct
purposes,— he is apt to find himself going the wrong way and life full of snares.

I enjoy the way my two boys speak of
my things as *ours*. They are only five
and seven, and their theology is yet very
crude. In a measure I stand in God's
place with them. They have things they
call their own,— some of their remote
ancestors must have been selfish,— but
they own my things, too. Perhaps after
fifteen or twenty years I will have them
better trained; but it is delightful now
to have them feel as if they owned me,
just as I feel that I own them. I will
lose something if we grow apart.

When a man has learned to join his
life to God's life, it changes his attitude
toward his fellows. One cannot recognize his relation and likeness to his father
without looking for the same traits in
others. Wherever we find men saying
"Our Father," we find them saying "My
brother" also. The two are inseparable.
This was Christ's way. He was with
people, busy with them,— not ostenta-

tiously measuring and calculating his
charity, but naturally, sharing their lives.
He did not say to a man, "Here am I, and
there are you; give me your burden and
I will bear it for you." He said, "Here
we are; take hold, and let us bear this
burden of ours." He and his gift were
never separated. He and the man he
was helping were always one. This
accounts for his self-forgetfulness. It is
a great thing to be unconscious of self in
one's work,— to throw ourselves under a
burden just as if we were some one else;
to identify ourselves and our beneficence
just as God does. This was Christ's way.
He told a story which illustrates it.
There were two boys in a family. Both
were selfish, and both planned to have a
good time. One took his share of his
father's goods and went away from home
and led a fast life. People said he went
to the bad. The other stayed at home
and saved. The good time he was planning for was in the future, when his
father was dead and he would have all.
One day the rake came home, spent,
wasted, humbled. The servants were

told to make a feast. The older brother was scandalized at his reception. "It is all right to be charitable," he said; "but I do not think he ought to be treated as a member of the family again. I think the father is too easy on him. I'll never let him forget that he is a reformed prodigal." But the father took the poor burned-out cinder of a life in his arms, and said, "My boy, my boy!"

This was Christ's way, and those who have caught his spirit are going about this world saying, "These children shall be my children; these men shall be my brethren." And this mothering and brothering of the race is the only way of helping it. One who has learned to know God in Christ's way loves others just as naturally as he loves himself.

Christ says, "I am the way." He means that his way is the way to live. Not the way to be religious. This was not a sermon, not said on Sunday. It was ordinary conversation about life. Christ was telling the way to live. Oh, how much we lose by making a mere preacher out of Christ! Religion and life are never

two separate occupations to the man who
carries his God around in his own heart.
You cannot take a mother and separate
her into her parts and say, "Here is a
child, here is a woman, here is the
motherhood." The dissection destroys
motherhood. So the separation of any
part of your life from your religion
destroys your religion by so much.
Christ's way — the complete identifica-
tion of himself and his God — is the
only true life. And life and religion
may be one.

You cannot live without a religion.
Many will try. Confusing religion and
belief, because they cannot believe as
other men do, they bundle all beliefs out
of doors and say they are not religious.
Do not follow these. When you are very
busy, your beliefs, like your clothes, will
wear out rapidly, and you will provide
yourself with new ones. But keep very
busy. I care less for what you believe
than for what you do. Religion is not
what men believe; that is philosophy.
Religion is what men do with their
beliefs —"emotion in action," Dr. Jordan

defines it. Now, every man has some central principle from which his emotions flow. With very many it is fear. With many more it is duty; the word *ought* becomes a kind of impersonal God, and sits in judgment over every act. With others it is avarice; they act because it will pay them either now or hereafter. With others still, it is love; all they do and plan is for others. They are as unreasonably unselfish about this as a mother in serving her child. But these are pleasant people, and one is sure to feel better who meets one of them. Christ was one of these. This was his way. All lovers of their fellows are Christians, too, and are saving their people by serving them. They may label themselves with some other title, but that makes little difference. Their reward is the same. They save men.

This is the test of any religion — its value as a social factor. Governor Stanford is quoted as saying, "Whichever form of religion furnishes the greatest comfort, the greatest solace, is the form that should be adopted, be its name what

it may." How shall we determine which
this religion is? By comparing the re-
ligions of the world? We can define
them, — Confucianism, Buddhism, Mo-
hammedanism, Zoroastrianism, or Juda-
ism. Surely, if splendid systems could
form a perfect life, these would furnish
them. But when we come to Christ, we
can make no definition. There is no
Christism. The so-called doctrines of
Christ are not new. But Christ is new.
With an egotism that would be despicable
if it were not divine, he boldly pushes
himself before his sayings, and says, "I
am the way." These others formulated
rules and precepts. Christ gave himself.
Living by rule and precept is tiresome and
discouraging. Personality is contagious.
It is the contagion of Christ's personality
that is conquering this world. Men
quarrel over Christianity, but Christ's
way is rapidly becoming the way of the
whole world; not only among those who
call themselves Christians, but among the
Jews and Mohammedans and Buddhists
as well, the leaven is working. It makes
the most of every man. It puts in every

man's hand the key to his own life. It points every man to the best and noblest in his own nature and says, "Here is your God-likeness,— feed it." It breaks down all barriers between man and his God. When this is true, it is of little consequence whether we label ourselves by one title or another. If you wish to bring the world to God, you cannot preach a theology and win. Go out and live God among your fellows, and they will be helped to live God, too.

It is this I now urge upon you: Choose Christ's way. Choose him. Go at the world in his way. In the laboratory and classroom, in the study, on the field, among your fellows during the idle hour as well as during that time every man ought to spend alone — make it all your Father's business. I ask you to begin this year of your college life as Christians. I do not define Christian. Do that for yourself. I do not ask you to surrender your individuality, except as individuality must forever be subservient to sociality. I lay down no conditions, nor require any tests other

c

than those you yourself create. I say
nothing about joining this church or
that. When you are at your work in the
world you will find that you amount to
more co-operating in an organization than
alone, and you will find one to your liking.

Look at Christ, and in your own way
be like him. You will find many pleasant companions going the same way.
Your own companionship will be pleasant
to you. Yonder in the forest I count
different kinds of vegetation by the score,
tall trees and clinging vines, shrubs and
nestling annuals, ferns and mosses in the
cañon, grasses and many-colored blossoms
in the open places,— each one searching
for its share of the same warm, bright
sunlight, and each making out of it its
best of its own kind. Consider these
lilies of the field; surely our Heavenly
Father feedeth them all. Be your best
self, and you will surely find God working with you. And you will understand
how Christ could say, "I and my Father
are one."

OUR FATHER

ONE day, when Jesus was talking about God to his disciples, Philip interrupted him, by asking, "Lord, show us the Father and we will be satisfied." And Jesus said to Philip, "Have I been so long time with you, and yet hast thou not known me?" "The Father and I are so mixed, so amalgamated, that my loving is his loving; my goodness, his goodness; my wisdom, his wisdom. I am in the Father and the Father in me, and all these works that I am doing, we — the Father and I — are doing. The words I speak and the works I do are his works and words."

This was the Master's way of quieting Philip's fears that he could not get near enough to God to feel at home with him. Jesus was *conscious* of God. He never defined him. He never sought to prove his existence or establish any doctrines

37

17032

about him.   He *assumed* God, and talked
about him as naturally as a boy talks
about his father.   When he was going
about doing good, he unquestionably recognized that God was doing the same;
so they worked together.   I have noticed
that a boy who occasionally takes hold
and helps me in something I am doing
does not first ask for proof that I am his
father, nor does he insist that some one
point out the family likeness.   He just
takes hold and helps, or imagines he
helps, and links himself to me by talking
a great deal about our work, and what we
are doing.   He just assumes that I am,
and that our life is one, as it is.   Now,
this is the way that Jesus always acts
toward God.   When he is working, he
expects God to co-operate, and he does.
When he is in trouble, he cries out for
help, and it comes.   When he is anxious
about leaving the crude and unripe disciples alone in the world, he talks the
whole situation over with his Father as
naturally as if they were sitting together
in the firelight before some family hearth-
stone.   This wonderfully successful and

ideal life that Jesus led received its whole explanation and impetus from this relationship between him and his God. We cannot read about it or study his life without believing that the relationship was real. Whether God did his part or not, we cannot escape the conclusion that Jesus lived and loved and served and died as he did because of his conviction that he and his Father were one,— one in spirit, in aim, in purpose. And when we think of the stupendous miracle of Christianity, when we see his principles abiding, his life and spirit going into all the dark corners of the world, we must believe that God was with him, and he knew it. It is that which "works," which stands the tests of time and place, which has God with it; and the everlasting life of Jesus is the strongest proof we could have that his method of conscious participation with God's life is the true way of living. But how often the cry comes from anxious and perplexed ones, "Oh, if I could only know God in this real, *personal* way, then I could live!" How many times I have been asked, "Show

me the Father, and I will be satisfied,"—
"Show me a personal God, and I will
pray to him!"   Dissatisfaction always
waits on the soul whose aspirations are
limited by its own sight and understanding.

Men may not all pray, but all men want
to pray.   Yet prayer is communion, and
is impossible unless two beings recognize common life as the basis of the
asking and giving.   So when people lose
the idea of a personal God they stop
praying.   When our intellects have ban-
ished God from his home in our hearts
and sent him out among the stars to build
and uphold things, then, however much
we may hunger for sympathy or need
help, we will not address our prayers to
the stellar spaces.   We can feel no fellowship or commonness with a being whose
business it is to make worlds out of
nebulæ, or who manifests himself as
gravitation or chemical affinity.   We can
know God only on ground common to
God and man; not on a plane of omnipo-
tence, for man is not omnipotent; not
on a plane of omnipresence, for man

is a little creature, and must stay close at home; but on a ground common to God, who makes and upholds *all* things, and *man*, who can make nothing, and upholds indifferently well. This must be man's ground. Notice how my boy and I meet and talk. I do not talk bionomics to him or expect him to talk about the laws of life to me. He does not dream of such things. They are my life. We talk about *his* things. A few weeks ago it was marbles, and I had to listen to "agates" and "comps," etc. Now it is tops, and I am learning over again the top vocabulary. I must, if I keep my dominion over him. "Tops" at present represents a part of our common ground. We live together there. We have other points where we meet. We sit in the same big chair before the fire, and talk at each other, he talking up to me, and calling me "Father," and I talking down to him such things out of my larger life as he will comprehend, planning to give him every good thing I can, and a few of the many things he asks for. But all the time it is his ground we

meet on.   Some day, when he has grown
up into my stature, we will talk face to
face, but now he finds me, if he finds me
at all, in his own heart and life.

Now, this common ground where we
meet — a fragment of my life, all of his —
is my life in him and his in me.   Here
love dwells; here is communion.   Here
we trade prayers for answers, knowledge
for ignorance, help for weakness.

Now, I want to teach a great lesson by
this homely illustration.   The illustration you can all understand, because you
have others like it in your own lives.
Such things have been with you always.
Have you not seen God in them?   When
Philip wanted to see God, Jesus pointed
to his own clean, strong, loving life and
said, "This is the Father in me."   So
I want to urge you to take out of your
commonest daily experiences the love that
is there, the kindness, the truth, the hunger for better things, the hatred for un-
clean things, all those aspirations that
draw toward a larger life, — away from
what you now are, toward what you would
be, — take all of these real *facts* out of

your life and name them " Father." When
you long for the sense of a personal God,
you mean that you want to feel that you
and God are alike, you want to draw on
him for help, and feel the help come.
You want to pray and talk over your life
with a real being like yourself, but strong,
not with an impersonal force. This is
just what Christ did. So real was God
to him that he called him *Father*, and
we can do the same. I do not hesitate a
moment to say that we can live as Jesus
did, immersed, consciously immersed, in
the presence of our Father; and this relation can be just as real and tender as that
between me and my boy. I am speaking
out of my own experience now; I know
what I am talking about.

I could construct a theistic argument.
I think I could satisfy your intellects, and
prove that we are being made in God's
image, that all that draws us toward better things is God's life in us. I think I
could prove this. I have done it for
myself; I think I could do it for you.
But it would still leave you unsatisfied.
You do not care to know that God is love

so much as you want to love God. I am
not appealing to your intellects this morning so much as to your affections.

Leave the attributes of God,— law,
power, eternity, wisdom,— leave those
three great impersonal *omnis*—omnipres-
ent, omnipotent, and omniscient—to your
intellect, and love God with your whole
heart at the same time you are loving your
neighbors. Do not think that you must
master a whole theological system before
you can commune with God. You talked
with your father, you called on him for
help, you worked with him and tried to
be like him long before you could spell
his name or comprehend his character. The understanding comes after the
fact.

Let me choose out of your lives some
of the real things, and ask you to interpret
them as I do in my own life. In the first
place, let us consider love. I choose this
because the deepest, tenderest experiences
of life are associated with it. The best
things that have come to you have been
brought by love, and you recognize yourself at your best when you are loving.

Do you remember some time when you were in trouble, when perhaps you went near to the brink of the valley of shadows, when your arm needed strength and your heart sympathy? And do you remember how they came? How strong hands gripped yours, how hearty words of cheer drove out your loneliness, how little acts multiplied, until you were surrounded by loving-kindness and tender mercies? We call this friendship. It is God abroad in his world. He that hath seen a friend hath seen God also. Do you remember those broken days of childhood, when you in many moods mixed good and bad in the mosaic of your growing life? When you were thoughtless, there was one who never forgot; when you were wrong, there was one who was always kind; when you were in tears, there was one who wept with you; when you rejoiced, there was one who was glad. You call this sacred friend "Mother." Is it possible that any of you have known a mother's love and yet know not God? He that hath seen a mother hath seen God also.

Or take, for illustration, *service:* iden-
tifying our lives with the lives of our
fellows and doing for them. As you have
seen wretchedness and misery or suffering, has your stronger nature been drawn
out to help and soothe until you have
forgotten, perhaps, your own ease and
comfort in your sympathy for another's
pain and sorrow? Thank your God
for manifesting himself through you.
These aspirations to help another are
the God-life in you. He that has felt
sympathy and served his fellows has
known God and manifested him.

And these yearnings for better things,
this longing for more life for yourself
and more happiness for others, this is
the beginning of prayer,—inarticulate,
dumb prayer, no doubt it often is,—but
cultivate it, give expression to it, and you
will find yourself depending more and
more on the sure return that comes
from every aspiration that rises toward
your Heavenly Father. Prayer is an
art to be cultivated. Men learn to talk
to the Father as they learn to speak
to one another. And men learn to listen

after they have learned to speak — to recognize and receive answers long after they have commenced to beg.

My friends, this is holy ground. Let me lead you reverently into my holy of holies and declare out of my daily experience that God hears and satisfies; that through these many channels, through friends and children and home, through those that give and those who receive, through the quiet breeze that blows after the heated day, through the triumph of righteousness and the pain of sin,— through all of these channels God speaks and reveals more and more of himself. And when I need him — and that is very often — my cry is heard, and in some good way answered. Through these same channels, by some of his many messengers, the answer comes. I am not always satisfied, for I want many things, but I am never deserted or allowed to feel alone if I wish the Father's presence.

Ye men of Stanford, I perceive that in all things you are somewhat religious. But you have reasoned about God's power and have studied his laws until you have ceased to feel your likeness to him, and have written over your altar the inscription, "To the unknown God." And the altar bears no sacrifice. What, therefore, ye worship as agnostics, declare I unto you, the God that made the world and all things therein, he, being Lord of heaven and earth, giveth to all life and breath and all good things, and is not far from each one of us. For in him we live and move and have our being. When man loves and serves, it is the child endeavoring to be like its father. When man longs for greater, nobler, truer things, it is the son recognizing his relation to the Parent.

Out of your lives take the love and sympathy, the purity, the truth, the tender things, and all that grows into larger life, and put these on the cold altar of your heart; then cut out those empty, lonely words, "To an unknown God," and write "Our Father." And bow before him; for this is your God, and he will not withhold any good thing from you if you walk uprightly.

Oft in the dusty course it seems
The face of Him I am to meet
Is dimmed before my straining eyes;
And silence answers to my cries—
Silence and doubt my questions greet.

Yet, pressing onward to my goal,
Some breeze will blow the dust apart.
'Tis dust my feet have raised that hides
The Father's smile that e'er abides.
The dust has changed, but not His Heart.

The silence is my ignorance
When reason seeks Him to define.
Life's mysteries are solved by life
And doubts that rise in anxious strife
Before the Love of God decline.

We seek in wordy phrase to paint
The Unknown God to finite eyes.
Our logic kills our charity,
Our wisdom widens mystery,
Our altars bear no sacrifice.

Yet to the listening ear God speaks
In myriad tongues on sea and shore,
In childish prattle, mothers' songs,
When prophets cry against men's wrongs,
Or love knocks at some prison door.

D

Faith born of love and fed by hope
Sees God where reason's eye is dim,
And reason led by faith will prove
So strong that doubts can never move,
Nor clouds disturb our trust in Him.

Then courage, fainting one, take heart;
Thy God in clouds hides not His face,
The veil is thine, thine is the fear,
Withhold thy cries, list to his cheer,
And onward press, fed by His grace.

OUR RELIGION

OUR RELIGION.

I HAVE recently read what was intended to be a criticism of the religious life of the University. It was written by one who evidently never graced the quadrangle with his presence or endangered his morality by listening to the lectures he stigmatized. Among his strictures were: "Confidently putting forth, as substitutes for religious belief, rank agnosticism and Darwinianism,"—"Belittling and often irreverent use of the Scriptures,"—"Evolution theories run wild," —"Elimination of the supernatural, and making natural science superior to revelation," etc.

It is but fair to say that we were made to share these sins with the State University, and that the article was written to persuade young men to go to another college, where they would not be exposed to such temptations, and where, as one of

them is quoted as saying, "he could be
a Christian, when he couldn't be one at
home."

I mention these criticisms not because
I am going to attempt to show that they
are not true, nor because I think it necessary to answer them. I think it well to
know what is said of us. It helps us to
prove the standards we have chosen to
live by. Moreover, I wish to warn you
against the possible danger of trying to
live up to our bad reputation. I have
noticed that a small boy, told that he is
a "bad boy," is apt to bristle with extem-
porized proofs of the truthfulness of your
statement. And I have noticed, too, that
men enjoy being called skeptics and heretics, and in these happy times, when there
is no danger from faggot or rack, a certain
kind of heresy is rampant, from motives
that seem akin to those that actuate a
rampant peacock.

For those who see in our Darwinianism deviltry, and who call our science
rank agnosticism, there is but one answer:
Let us make this altar the center and
source from which true men and women

shall go into the world to live the pure, true life that Christ led. Let us multiply helping hands and fit men to save their fellows in the wasteful battle of life.

There [pointing to picture of Christ] is our ideal,—a man who dared live *true*, though he was called heretic and traitor and devil; who lived his simple, human, godlike life, though his church excommunicated him, his friends deserted him, his people killed him; and who stands to-day with one hand on our Father's throne and one on the pulse of humanity,—our hero, our ideal, our Saviour. Let us live his life among men, and they will stop talking about us and worship him.

But while we are none of these bad things that good people in their ignorance call us, there is that about the University which makes the four years you spend here a danger period in your lives. We are not so bad as we are painted, and yet from the standpoint of certain people we are a great deal worse than they dream us to be.

In the first place, we *think* here,—

think about things that are never questioned in some places. Thinking is a
dangerous pastime; try it carefully and
see. Many things that we imagined we
believed will not stand the test of thought.
You will realize, as you never did before,
the danger of accepting things without
thinking, of not proving all things. You
will find that you have been holding fast
to much that is not good. It will cost
you time and many heartaches to transfer
your allegiance from external idols and
images to internal convictions. But when
you have accomplished it, you will think
it worth all it cost. Men who have found
themselves have found their God; they
live like the stars, shining by their own
living light.

" Unaffrighted by the silence round them,
     Undistracted by the sights they see,
   These demand not that the things without
        them
        Yield them love, amusement, sympathy.

"And with joy the stars perform their
        shining
     And the sea its long moon-silvered roll,

For self-poised they live, nor pine with
    noting
All the fever of some differing soul."

In the next place, we are separated
here from real living — isolated. We are
receiving, and not giving. Even the best
education has in it this element of inac-
tivity which leads to a certain kind of
degeneration of a part of our nature
while we are developing and training
another. A man is only safe when he is
giving himself to others. This is a period
of accumulation. It is an expensive process. It costs more than the money
necessary to pay our board-bills and buy
our books. It costs a part of our power
of giving. The unused function of giving weakens and would disappear if we
stayed as students too long. It will
return when we get to work among men
again. But we do not always recognize,
as we should, that we get out of relationship with our fellows during this time of
preparation for better work among them.

I have heard people mourn because
students lose their enthusiasm for reli-

gious work while at college. It is unavoidable. And no student should write
himself down as a backslider because he
cares more for his themes than he does
for his committee work in Christian Endeavor. You cannot grind your ax and
chop with it at the same time. I have
noticed that farmers lose their enthusiasm
for the plow when sitting at the dinner-
table. But when digestion has waited
on appetite the plow regains its charms.
Let us use our common sense here. You
are preparing for life; you are not living.
I have heard some of you pray that your
waning interest in religious work might
be revived, and this while you are struggling with fifteen or eighteen hours of
university work. Your business here is
to study, to religiously study, to study
Greek or history or science, in order that
you may do better religious work when
you go out. To try to maintain your effi-
ciency in Christian Endeavor or church
work while you are at the same time trying to train yourself for living is to make
a jack of all trades of yourself and a
master of none.

But be careful here. Do not allow yourself to think that you are ceasing to be religious because you are giving less time to prayer-meetings and more to lectures and laboratories. The study of God's works at any time — providing they are recognized and studied as the works of God — is religion. David was as religious when he lay among his flocks and saw that the heavens declare the glory of God, as when he was chopping up Philistines, or asking God to destroy his enemies. I would like to wipe out this misleading conception, still fostered by some who should condemn it, that certain occupations are sacred, and others are secular, and therefore profane.

Nothing that a clean, pure man can do is unreligious. I do not hesitate to say that the highest duty you can perform while a student here is to honestly, prayerfully, and in the fear of God, pile up your one hundred and twenty hours of credit and keep out of the hands of the Committee on Doubtful Cases. That is what you are here for. If you have any time left when you have done this,

then work along what you are pleased to
call a distinctively religious line, but do
not write anathema after your name if it
takes most of your time to keep up with
your work. It makes little difference
what names others call you. If you are on
good terms with yourself and your God,
rest there. Do not confine your praying
to your closets. Do some of it at the
study-table, on the athletic field, and in
the recitation-room. It is wonderful how
much the Father is concerned in *all* our
activity, if we only open our eyes to see.
And remember that a certain amount of
intellectual and spiritual disorder is sure
to come while you are isolated from real
living in this protected spot where the
opportunities for receiving will always be
greater than those for giving out.

This disturbance is part of the price
of your education. When you are out
among people again, the balance will be
readjusted; and if you have been faithful
here, your devotion will welcome any
field of action there.

The church and most religious work is
not yet adjusted to college life. The

church is a social institution, doing a work among men that no other institution can do, and it is adjusted to the social life. In proportion as our life here differs from the life of the world, then, are we out of touch with the church. It is still necessary for a student to take a kind of furlough if he wishes to do much work in any of these organizations, which, nevertheless, exercise a certain kind of extra-territorial jurisdiction over his conscience and his religion. I have worked in church schools and state schools, and those like our own, which are neither, and this is true of them all. It will last until the Church widens her definition of service to include those who study God's works, and until the school recognizes worship as a part of its legitimate exercise.

I have one other thought, and it concerns us all, students, and teachers, and friends. I refer to the tendency we share in common with all great educational institutions of our time, to emphasize the intellectual and suppress the emotional side of our natures.

A wise man said many years ago that faith without works is dead. He meant that a religious life that did not bear fruit in good deeds was no life at all, and not religious. A recognition of this, and the overdevelopment of the sterily emotional side of religion, has led many thoughtful people to turn away from the religious organization and to welcome the increasing opportunities for social service. The new science of sociology has set people to thinking about methods, to talking about service, and to seeking for ways of helping their fellows. I think this longing to be of use to their fellows is stronger among men than ever before. The fact that the churches still give more attention to man's future condition and less to the present adds to this divergence. There are hundreds of people to-day who are doing splendid work for their fellows, helping them to larger, more abundant life, who hardly ever enter a church or feel the need of its services.

Now, here is a serious danger. Religion has in it two elements,—one is worship, the other is service,—a God side and a man side. It is possible for men to give so much time to the God side of religion—to worship, to praying, to diving into the heavenly depths for beatific visions—that they become absolutely useless to their fellows. Most of you will grant this, because this tendency is what most of you criticise in the churches.

Now, I wish to make another statement. It is possible for men to become so methodical and intellectual in the service of their fellows that they lose the power of sympathy and love. Service to our fellows alone is not religion any more than slavish toil is love. Religion engages the affections of men. It unites us to our fellows, not because it is a dictum of sociology to be altruistic, but because we love them as ourselves.

Now, love is the ground common to God and man. Love is where they meet, —the only place where they can meet face to face,—just as a mother and child meet and understand each other on the common plane of their mutual love. On this plane the mother shares her larger

life according to the child's capacity:
that is her *beneficence;* and on this plane
the child yields allegiance to the ideal
she partially sees in the parent above
her: this is her worship.

Suppose there are other children in the
family. Their mutual love and service
and homage to the kind one above them,
combined with parental care and sympathy, make that incarnation of heaven on
earth — a home. A house, a mere house
where people bearing the same name sit
down to eat together three times a day,
where service is rendered from policy or
duty or pay, is not a home — just a
boarding-house. It takes love to make
a home. And in just the same way it
takes love to make any part of this universe heaven. For love is self-surrender,
and religion includes this element of self-
surrender. Just as love unites the parent
and child and leads to union and co-
operation and fellowship, so love unites
God and man, and this union is a vital
element in religion.

It includes worship, because it looks
up to a higher power and seeks to fellow-

ship with it. Morality and duty are both
included, but they are swallowed up by
love. But the great vitalizing element
that gives strength to faith and life to
duty is the consciousness that God is
working with us as we serve our fellows,
and that we can love him. Now, those
of you who are serving your fellows are
only claiming one half of your reward,
unless you are conscious of fellowship
with the Father in your service. You are
as a servant in the family where you
might be a child.

This is one of the dangers of student
life — to substitute sociology, or, worse
still, ethics, for religion. Sociology is
not religion any more than the study of
tactics is war. The soldier does not gain
confidence and trust in his commander
by studying the rules of war. After being led to victory after victory he gains
that reverence for his leader which, combined with his study and drill (that is,
his sociology and ethics) and with his
experience, makes him invincible. So
we, working together with God in the
regeneration of this world, gain that

personal relation to him which gives meaning to our work and inspiration to our lives.

Let us, then, worship God; as we love our neighbors as ourselves, let us also love God with all our heart and soul and mind.

Sympathy is shallow unless combined with reverence; works are but temporal unless nurtured by faith in the eternal; service is tiring unless fed by worship; and man is an enigma unless he knows God.

NEW WINE AND OLD
BOTTLES

WHAT is our greatest danger? Perhaps it is the danger of failing to live true. I do not mean hypocrisy,—that is acting a lie,—but the failure to put into action what we are.

Here is a common saying: "This is my ideal; I confess I do not live up to it." And this often means, "I do not try." If I were talking to students of zoology I would say that the presence of any power or organ means that it is being used; its disappearance means that it is being neglected. All the symmetrical forms and all the grotesque and one-sided forms are the products of this law. And we are under this law. Its action is rapid in the immaterial world. The removal of undesirable things, and the making permanent of good things, are never to be regretted; but by failing to live our ideals, we lose the best part of ourselves.

69

We hear much in this place about the dangers that threaten the young in the University. Parents and friends anxiously watch the changes that come, and fear the end. College life means metamorphosis, and each stage is fraught with danger. Those who anxiously watch the process wonder how it is possible to get an image of a man from the grotesque forms that sometimes masquerade as youth. Of course, the man comes, in most cases. College life is not a failure, though it is far from the success it might be. The intellectual and spiritual birth-rate exceeds the death-rate. Few fail utterly; few succeed in any great degree; but the balance is on the side of success.

When a young man enters college most of his standards are external. Few of those who come here have lived long enough to accumulate much experience. The training of early years gives a trend which none of us are strong enough to overcome completely, even when we recognize its desirability. Our opinions, our beliefs, our bias in social and political and intellectual questions are derived from our parents far more completely than our forms and features. It is perhaps the knowledge of this fact that adds to the solicitude of parents when they send their children away from home. They know what the student does not find out until later,— that this training has never been tested by the one whom it most concerns, that the standards are external, and that opinions are not yet convictions.

Now, it is here, during this period of intellectual living, that the change comes in our attitude toward our standards of living. Heretofore we have lived as others directed or influenced. We are here to acquire the power of directing ourselves. Impulse and feeling and emotion must here acquire some rational basis. Up to this time they have been the spontaneous fruits of our living. Heretofore we have acted because we felt like it; now we must know why we act.

This analytical process destroys much of our power of doing. By the time we have studied our steam to find what it is, it has become cold water. By the time we have thought much about the emotional and impulsive religious life which we have led, the emotion is all gone, or it may be that it is displaced by another. Cold water that has once been steam is insipid and somewhat disgusting. And so a religious life that has cooled down from emotionalism into rationalism often gives its owner a feeling akin to nausea. Some of the hardest words I have ever heard spoken against religion have come from those who at one time were enthusiastically religious. Some new wine has been poured into old bottles and turned sour.

Our beliefs grow up with us. They are not entirely, not even largely, a matter of the intellect. They are part of our breeding and of our living. Many of our reasons for things are inherited from our parents. We do not always understand how they are constructed. Like a child who has received a watch, we play with it and break it, but cannot mend it. Many people think children ought not to play with watches. They are for older people. In the same way many people think that children should not play with reason, or meddle with the carefully constructed thought-systems of their fathers. They want them to take these systems, use them, call them their own, but dread the analyzing spirit that may try to find how the thing is made, and so spoil it.

Many fathers and mothers say to me, "If my boy will only hold on to the *fundamentals*." They are afraid that the business of the University is to overthrow fundamentals. As if fundamentals could be overthrown! What they mean by fundamentals is their own conception of the truth, the basis of their own belief. They want their boys to wear their clothes,—not the same style only, but the identical clothes,—with all the creases and wrinkles and patches in place. Now, the wrinkles and creases represent experience and testing, and the patches are the scars—honorable scars of victory. And I have no patience with the sophomoric spirit which vaunts its reason and throws into the rag-bag everything that the

fathers believed. We would not be here
to-day if our fathers had not believed
very close to the truth. However far
afield we may go in our young and cal-
low days, the larger part of us will be
found revamping the old beliefs of our
fathers and mothers when we go to work
on the world. I have taught long enough
to know that this is true. But the time
comes when the child becomes the man,
when he must know how his watch is made,
even if it costs him several watches to find
out,—the information is worth several
watches. The time comes when he finds
himself asking, "Why do I believe this?
Why do I practice this?" And because
he cannot at once find a reason that will
satisfy, many of the things he has believed all his life in common with his
father will be laid on the shelf until the
experiences of life lay a foundation for
them again. Then they will be taken
down. He will cease to do many of the
things he has customarily done, because
he finds that they are not the natural
fruit of his life. It seems like hypocrisy
to do them, even for the sake of father

and mother. I have letters and figures from some hundreds of students that show me that eighty-five per cent. of them take up their old practices again when their real living seeks expression. But there is nothing unnatural or very alarming to me in the suspension of religious activity, which is common among young men and women at the University. It is one of the penalties we pay for our isolation. Student life is not real life. It is a dangerous period,— all climacteric periods are dangerous. But they seem to be part of the plan of God's world. This suspension is only temporary. It is largely due to the confusion of change and readjustment; to the transfer of allegiance from authority to self. The change rarely comes without confusion, but it must come, and when it is complete it is worth all it costs. A little bit of real living will bring back the enthusiasm and emotion, and no one can be faithful and true to his ideals without finding God displacing them with himself. Much as I sympathize, therefore, with the more or less painful processes of change, I do

not regard the change itself as the greatest danger that threatens the young man
or woman here. It must come, and this
is the natural time for it to come.

To the one who looks in vain among
his books and notes for the old standards
by which he shaped his life, I would say,
"They are not there. You are here to
study tools and methods, and this study
fills a large part of your life. But the
study of tools and methods and the filing
of your wits will neither give you the
glow of exercise nor the emotions of living; nor will study about God ever give
you the confidence that working with him
gives." As students our position is ab-
normal. We get more than we give.
When you resume your place in the
world, life will bring back the emotion
you think you have lost, and clear up all
the doubts that now seem so great. We
all face the danger of mistaking the form
in which the truth was clothed for the
truth itself.

Calvinism and Arminianism are trifling
matters compared with the fact that God
is and that we may call him our Father.

Unitarianism, Trinitarianism are mere word-quibbles compared with the fact that the spirit of Christ is in the world, saving it. These things are not fundamental. They are what many mean by essential and fundamental, but they are only *terms*, forged by human intellects to express one phase of the truth as it appeared to them. There will be some astonished people who reach heaven and find that Christ was neither Methodist nor Presbyterian, Calvinist nor Arminian — that he cared for none of these things except as they hampered and hindered those who believed them instead of believing him, who worshiped them instead of using them to serve him.

.   .   .   .

Many of you are now in a period of change. Well that it should come during the isolation of your college days. You will never have so much time to settle things as now; yet you will find that you can settle very few. Have confidence in yourself. Trust your nerves to tell the truth, unless you have been abusing them. Some state this another way, and say,

"Trust in God." I mean the same thing. Be sure that you believe, and do not hold a mere opinion. To define is not belief; experience gives belief.

God and righteousness and Christ, miracles and immortality, fatherhood and brotherhood, sin and redemption, these are not theological words, though many theologies have been written about them. All are facts of experience, and as facts they all touch our lives in some way. Our touch with them is our knowledge of them. But do you not see it? We cannot talk about them and compare notes about them without changing our ideas of them and modifying our definitions.

Many think it impossible to separate these things from the philosophy about them, wicked to try. We must try. We will ask Christ and history and literature and life what they say about these great facts. When we get their answers, for they all speak of them, we will probably construct another philosophy in place of the old. It will seem better to us than the old, though perhaps not very different, because it expresses things that we believe, not what we have been told to believe.

Believe in yourself. If a statement or a fact appeals to you as true, believe it. Be your own authority. Bottle your own wine. Friends will stand around with old bottles and beg you to put your new wine in them. They are wrong in asking, and you are wrong to try. Your new wine needs aging. It must be worked over and must swell up and settle down and be tested to see if it is worth anything before it can be put in anything but a new, elastic bottle. Bottle it for yourself. It is the best wine in the world for you. Perhaps when it has aged it will be just like that in the old bottles, but you must cling to it as it is. It is yours.

So I ask you not to be afraid of the fruit of your own thoughts. We here study together these great truths of life,— God and Christ and man, sin and life and death and immortality. It is far more important that you should be sincere with yourself than that you should believe something that somebody has told you.

There is no final test of truth but this one — its appeal to our lives. Coleridge says somewhere that the pre-eminence of the Bible lies in the fact that it finds us. By this test judge all truth,— does it *find* you? Do not wait to reason it out. The fundamentals, the real fundamentals —the basis of all belief—cannot be reasoned out.

The fatherhood of God, the divinity of man, the reality of righteousness, the spiritual life, immortality, the ideality of Christ,— these are some of the fundamentals. We apprehend them. Just as we get up in the morning and throw open the blinds and *know* that the sun is there, so these great facts appeal to us when we squarely face them. But the greatest danger that may threaten a young man or woman is the failure to put into action the truth he does believe.

I sat by the side lines the other evening when the ball was driven almost to my feet, and those twenty-two demons whose breathing nearly burst their canvas sides stood puffing a moment before they sprang at each other's throats. I almost stampeded; I did long to be one of them again. But I only sat and shivered there on the bleachers with another football philosopher, and we told each other how to play the game.

A young man said to me the other day, "I have not been in church for three years." I looked him over as a curiosity and asked him why. His reply was, "The glaring inconsistencies of church members made me sick. I could not stand it and just stayed away." How consistent! Here was such a good church member that he never went to church. A man who imagined he had an ideal standing with his back to it. Ideals are to run races with. The moment we stop chasing them they sit down — become opinions.

If the old channel through which your best life flowed is filled up, find another one. If you cannot put your new wine into old bottles, find new ones. Bottle it or lose it. If you cannot serve God and man through the church or Christian Endeavor because the inconsistencies there *glare* at you, let your truth *glare*

F

somewhere that men seeing how consistent a man can be, may be led to think how true God is. If you have new light on old questions, let that light shine. If you put it under a bushel it will go out. "If therefore the light that is in thee be darkness, how great is that darkness."

The time comes more than once in a man's life when he must know what he believes, when the truth that is in his own heart is all that he can find. But no truth is ours until we first live it, until it enters into our lives and we become it.

THANKSGIVING

THANKSGIVING.

AT their best the lives of men are but the lives of children; God must view them as such. To him our wisdom must be foolishness; our strength, weakness; and our best endeavor crude and incomplete.

I have watched children at their play. Everything they do willingly is play; they groan and fret over things they do not like to do, and make burdens of them. But the things they do gladly fill their lives so full they can see nothing else, and they leave undone many things they ought to do, and would suffer for their lack if loving hands did not do for them. All day long they play, planning much that is never done and doing much they never planned, happy so long as they are busy, and busy until sleep snatches them from the midst of a bedtime romp, unconscious of their sleepiness.

They may not know that their play
is directed and controlled. They think
little of the love that guards and guides.
They toil not, and yet they are fed; they
spin not, and yet are clothed. Almost
unconscious of the great father-and-
mother world, in the midst of which
they live, they know it only where it
touches their immediate needs, or seems
to interfere with their desires. They
never know how much more they receive than they earn, or how much less
they suffer than they deserve. Love they
know, but only its smiling face. They
have not yet identified it with self-
sacrifice.

They have their sorrows; for loss and
gain, seed-time and harvest are never
separate from life, and these sorrows
seem very big, and fill their whole world
full of tears. For, child-like, they do
not realize that the tears are in their
eyes alone, nor do they know that the
kind heart, above which their despair lies
helpless, already has new joys and larger
life to occupy them. It does not make
the pain hurt less to be told that it will

not last, and the child cannot understand
how it can live without that which it has
lost. But the mother understands for it,
and has already provided other things
to fill the life that is emptied of all but
memory. And the mother is not surprised
to see smiles returning through the tears,
and the baby's face, a little older for its
grief, contented again.

So children live and move and have
their being in a world of love which they
hardly know and never understand until
they themselves become the love that surrounds and blesses other lives. Blessed,
thrice blessed is the man who has awakened into the likeness of his father and
his mother, and still has them with him
to receive the burden of his gratitude.

Life is a parable, and they who know
it best see in its tenderest relations the
key to the eternal mysteries of God. Are
we not, at our very best, but children in the
dark, short-sighted, self-centered, filled
with our own affairs, unconscious of the
Providence that surrounds us, more conscious of our losses than of our blessings, and receiving more than we can give

away. Does not God look at us as we overlook our children,— planning and leading, doing for us the things that we leave undone to our hurt, "preventing us by the blessings of his goodness"? Do we not understand him best when we put aside our definitions and dogmas and cry "Father"?

It is for this glimpse of God that Thanksgiving days come. Every life should have many of them. Not that we should work ourselves into a state of blind optimism by enumerating our blessings, and blindly refusing to see our sorrows. We cannot understand God fully except through the medium of sorrow. And these blessings, of which we all can name so many, are not a salve to deaden pain, but strength to help us bear it.

The feeling above all others that should possess us to-day is, that in this busy world we are, after all, at home with our Father, watched over and guided and blest just as we used to be in that other home where love withheld so many things that we wanted and gave so much more than we needed.

Do you remember in the "Bonnie Brier Bush" how Carmichael preached his first sermon? It was the evangel of the Lord Jesus. He and his people were together caught up into the higher heaven, and the orphaned boy saw there something that made him hurry home and throw himself on his aunt's shoulder crying, "Oh, Auntie, if she could have been there!" That was Carmichael's thanksgiving. Through the first-fruit of his life he began to know his mother.

So we, as we grow older and wiser, turn from the plaudits of our friends and praise our Heavenly Father; so we drop our garnered treasures and lift our empty hands in gratitude to him who made the harvest possible; so we link our lives with our Father's in everything we do, and see that his love is making our life possible in greater and greater fullness; so we come to see that all our time and business, our friends and our power, our stores and our knowledge, our joys and our sorrows, our failures and our victories, are all a part of the great home-making of which our good Father is the center.

This is why thanksgiving is healthful
and meet. We learn to know God in
the only way man can ever know him,—
through the recognition of his great love
and many blessings.

It is the selfish child who forgets to
say "Thank you." Generous natures say
it easily. Those who are doing most for
their fellows are those whose hearts are
full of gratitude. Some of you may say
this morning, "I have no part in this
service; I am here as a spectator; this is
not my thanksgiving." Is it not because
you are not helping God make a home
for the men and women in this world that
you do not see how much he has done for
you? Like that young man who took his
possessions into the far country, you are
out of the Father's reach and cannot know
his kindness, and you have little or nothing left to give. Come back home! Take
hold and help the Father in his home-
making, and you will grow to know him
so well as you work together, giving
more abundant life to your fellows, that
your heart will overflow with praise and
thankfulness to him who has given you

a part in a life so glorious. "Beloved, now are we the sons of God, and it doth not yet appear what we shall be; but we know that when he shall appear we shall be like him, for we shall see him as he is."

LIBERTY

LIBERTY.

"If the Son therefore shall make you free, ye shall be free indeed."

THE history of man is a story of a struggle for freedom. Oppression is one cause of every war, love of freedom the other. Ages before Pharaoh made the lives of the Israelites bitter with hard bondage, the slave had cried out with the weight of his chains. The moan of the oppressed, the clank of his bonds, the harsh voice of the cruel taskmaster form an unbroken monotone in the midst of which History's obligato is often nearly drowned.

And the heaviest chains have not always been of iron. Superstition and ignorance have held men captive, and conscience, always in advance of man's development, has cut deeper than the oppressor's lash.

Men have never been free. They have broken through dungeon walls to find other wider walls around them. Knowledge reveals ignorance, and righteousness makes sin most hideous. Put your ear against the bosom of humanity at any time and interpret the secret of its throbbing prisoner, and you find the hope of freedom back of all its struggles,—freedom from hunger, from poverty, from suffering or pain, from ignorance or fear, freedom from appetite and avarice and passion and its own baser nature. And this hope, so large a part of man's nature, the strongest incentive to struggle and growth, has been fed and nourished by prophet and priest. The goal of all the ages has been liberty. Christ's first sermon proclaimed deliverance to captives and liberty to them that are bruised.

Man is made to resent oppression. He can be led better than he can be driven. It is his God-given independence, not sin, which causes his whole nature to array itself against a command. Fear is not a good master. It never breeds love. Man can never be happy unless he does what he wants to do. A perfect man cannot be made by the Ten Commandments. "Thou

shalt not do" often makes man want to
do. God made man independent and with
a will, and made his will free—allowed
him to do as he pleases. And when
we come to him, he does not wish us
to pluck out our wills and throw them
away, and come to him as slaves, as
human machines. He wants men, men
who have wills, men who are free, men
who can do as they please—men who
please to come to him. And Christ recognized man's nature, his Godlike power
of willing, when he wrote across the
decalogue the single word LOVE, which
forever blotted out the command and
substituted an entreaty. "Thou shalt"
and "Thou shalt not" became "Come
unto me." Instead of sitting afar off in
the heavens and trying to reform men
from the outside in, to drive them by
fear and duty, the Almighty Ruler
revealed his love through Jesus Christ
and came down to our level and lived
our life, and setting his face heavenward
he said: "Follow me. I am the way,
the truth, and the life. Ye shall know
the truth, and the truth shall make you

free. If the Son therefore shall make you free, ye shall be free indeed."

What is it to be free? What is the freedom which Christ offers?

I stood one sunny day on a coral reef in the harbor of Vera Cruz. The hazy blue air was full of sunshine and the healthy odors of the sea. Birds were tumbling about overhead in the perfect abandon of strength and room and tropical comfort. The white rocks and blue sea were mixing in a line of fleecy foam until the coral seemed to flow away on the wave crests. It was a perfect day, such as God sends us often when he lets heaven down to rest on earth for a little while. At my feet was a square hole cut out of the rock. Across it were bars of iron. I put my face down, and when my eyes became accustomed to the darkness below, I could see human forms there,— men in chains, standing in water ankle-deep, with the ocean ceaselessly pounding overhead, its hoarse laugh reminding them that they would be thrown to the sharks when they were dead. I could see their haggard faces turned up toward

the little barred square of light, which
was all of the great free outside world
they could see. Since that day that Mexi-
can prison has been the background
against which I have set my ideal of
freedom. Chained hand and foot, in-
closed by rocky walls, dependent upon
their masters for food and drink and air
and life, these men were slaves.

And yet not all slaves are in chains or
behind prison bars. Standing beside me
in the group that looked into that dismal
hole was a young American. He seemed
free. He could go where he pleased. He
could gratify his appetites and desires.
He was on his way to his Northern home
to wed a pure-hearted girl who was waiting for him there. He read me from one
of her letters, and one could see that he
was her ideal of manhood. Yet the
night before he spent in a Vera Cruz
brothel. The purity he was taking home
to his betrothed was only acted. His
manhood was only on the surface. The
truth was not in him. He was not what
he seemed to be. He was afraid lest he
should seem to be what he was. He was

chained by his sins and imprisoned by
the wall of falsehood he had built around
himself until he could walk the paths of
truth only in great fear lest the rattle of
his secret chains would reveal his cap-
tivity.

A man is not always free when he
seems to do as he pleases. It depends
upon what he pleases to do. Nor are
outward chains the only badge of slavery.
It is true that wherever Christ has gone,
emancipation has followed. "Imperial-
ism has given way to democracy, and
slavery to free labor." Peter slept in
prison, and an angel came and set him
free; but this is not the way Christ's
freemen are liberated. No angel touches
the sleeping prisoner that the chains may
drop from his galled wrists, but a divine
strength has been imparted to the bond-
man until, like Samson, he has risen from
his slumber and shaken himself, and his
withes have parted like tow in the flames.
The reformation of Christ has been
peculiar in this. It has reformed men by
making them strong enough to reform
themselves. The angel came in the night

and touched Peter, and his chains fell off
and he was free. This is the old way of
liberating. The spirit of Jesus Christ *in*
Paul made him victor over his own baser
nature, and set him free from the despo-
tism of his own folly and the mastership
of the Evil One. That is Christ's way.
His reformation is from the inside out.
Man becomes a partner in the process.
And though the reformation is from
within, man has not that within him
which can effect it. It must be imparted
from without. It is God-given. Have
you ever tried self-reformation? Have
you ever tried by taking thought to add
one cubit to your stature? To lift yourself by the hair of your head? Have
you ever on January first resolved to cast
away the old sin that has so long tyran-
nized you and made you its slave? And
have you on January second seen the
tempter dangling the old sin, which he
had caught? And as he held it before
you, you have tried to look away, and
have put out your hand to push it away,
but have grasped it instead and brought
it to your bosom and embraced it there.

Have you known what it is to cry out, like Paul, "O wretched man that I am! who shall deliver me from this body of death?" That which is so hard, even impossible for you, is made easy for you by Christ. He displaces your weakness by his might, and whom he makes free is free indeed. A physician in Illinois claims to have discovered a medicine which when given to a drunkard will make him loathe alcohol. Our Great Physician imparts to us his own nature, and we hate sin as he hated it.

By far the severest struggles of men for liberty have been against sin and un-righteousness,— severest because they have been secret. The battle has been fought alone. No touching of elbows and bracing of shoulders and strength of comradeship, which add so much to man's power of standing before the missiles of the enemy; but instead the still hours of a sleepless night, or, alone in the multi-tude, behind the thin mask we put on over our sins because we are ashamed of them. Men always *try* to do right. It is not natural for man to sin. He is made to be free, and the chains of sin gall as much as chains of iron. In the heart of every man four motives drive toward righteousness — fear, duty, hope, and love. He tries to do right because he is afraid of the punishment of wrong-doing, or because he feels that he ought to do right, or because he hopes for the reward of right-doing, or because he loves to do right. Three of these motives are poor masters. Christ's motive is by far the best one.

The man who does right because he is afraid of punishment is not free. The man who will not steal because he sees the prison bars is a thief nevertheless. The man who is set free from drink by a policeman standing guard over each saloon is not free indeed. Nor does it matter what form the restraint takes. Fear is always a master, and he who fears is always a slave. If you are honest because it is the best policy, your honesty is assumed, not real. If you attend church because it is respectable, the church is your prison, and public opinion your jailer. If you walk the

strait path when with your wife or
neighbor, when away from their protec-
tion you will probably attend the theater
instead of the church, and indulge the
appetite from which shame or fear alone
defended you.

The motive of duty is higher, but far
from perfect. Moreover, it is a cold,
heartless master. Do you love your wife
because it is your duty? Are you kind
to your neighbor because you ought to
be? Do you try to hold appetite and
passion and desire in check because you
are morally obliged to? You are like
that one-talent man who brought to his
Lord his debt of duty, and lost principal
as well as interest and received no word
of commendation.

Some men do right because of the
hope of reward. The delights of the
Eternal City are always before them.
They try to hate this world and all it
contains of opportunity and training.
They try to buy their way to heaven by
deeds of righteousness. This is merce-
nary. Do you remember the young man
who came to Jesus by night? He had

put the tables of stone in one pan of the balance, and hoped to see Eternal Life rise in the other. From his youth up he had been working for a reward, yet the first command to *love* sent him away sorrowing.

Christ offers the freedom of love. He does not demand a service of fear. Perfect love casts out fear. He does not demand a service of duty. That which the law could not do in that it was weak, the spirit of life in Christ Jesus hath made us free from. Indeed, Christ demands no service whatever. We are no longer servants, but friends. We are adopted. We become members of God's family, and therefore his work is our work. We do right because we please to do right. He changes us into his image so that we hate sin and love righteousness.

The service of love does not question —does not count the cost. There is no friction in love. It requires no process of cold reasoning to make you cherish your mother or your wife. You never think of service when making your child

happy. Love hides reason, and crowds
out even the thought of sacrifice. Love
makes it possible for us to grow without
taking thought, makes righteousness natural, makes us free indeed.

"I am the way, the truth, and the
life. . . . And ye shall know the truth,
and the truth shall make you free."

FRAGMENT

FRAGMENT.*

A VERY large part of the intellectual class finds itself to-day between the horns of a dilemma. On the one hand, the mind is dominated by inheritance and training until it identifies religion with its institutions, its dogmas, its forms, its figures of speech; on the other, this mind is trained by the methods and literature of the age to war with the institutions of religion, to ignore her forms and reject her dogmas. The dilemma is not a new one, though its present dimensions belong to the latter half of this century.

By this dilemma one who would be religious is tempted to separate his religion from his intellectual life to the great disturbance of the former, or to close his eyes to what they see and distrust reason and experience so far as they lead him away from his faith. This is a form of

* Written probably in November or December, 1898, but not delivered.

intellectual dishonesty not so common now as a few years ago. By this same dilemma one who would be rational is tempted to hoodwink himself by imagining that he believes what he knows he doubts, or to classify himself as unreligious altogether because he is not like some people, who say they believe what he must doubt, and who loudly affirm their own religion. The dilemma is not a new one, but to those whose expanding intellectual life leads them to it for the first time it is new and very real. Of these there are many in our midst. I speak chiefly for these.

I believe that every man can and ought to be religious. I do not think he is a complete man until he is religious. If you will accept my definition of religion, you will think so too. I cannot make you religious. I would not if I could. That is your part. Being is not born of hearing, but of doing. But I have learned some things in my experience with young men and women that have been very helpful to me and to others to whom I have given them. Some of these things I bring to you, hoping they may be needed. I like to bring to this chapel platform the best my life gives me, and the best thing out of my experience is that the life Jesus Christ lived is the best life for any man or woman. People do not readily believe this. When we remember how quickly men throw away old things for newer and better, how rapidly new inventions are adopted the world over, we can but wonder that the best life has so slowly commended itself to the race. But I think we are beginning to see that the world has had but imperfect and few glimpses of the real life of Jesus. An artificial, man-made Jesus, constructed of Greek philosophy, Oriental mysticism, and Roman legalism, has grown up between the real Jesus and a harassed people who yet instinctively feel that there is a living being within the mass of stuff associated with his name.

With most people to-day the terms Christianity and Religion are synonymous. Even the Jew of to-day will speak of the civilization which he himself has so well helped to build as a Christian civilization. The adjective Christian and the term Christianity are used to designate and define that movement which, wider than any church, broader than any creed, has carried our moral and social and intellectual life far in advance of that of any other age. Even men who would rather believe like Buddha or Confucius prefer to *live* like Christians. Christianity is one of the very few universal things in the world to-day, until we seek to define it—then Babel ensues. Now, the reason for this confusion and lack of agreement is the fact that men do not base their definitions upon the reality, but upon deductions and doctrines which from their very nature can never be tested by experience.

This confusion of tongues has turned many true men and women away from Christianity. Go to them and say, in Jesus' name, "Well done, good and faithful servant; you are a Christian." And they will answer, "I never was baptized, never joined the church, never recited the creed, and never said, Lord, Lord." Then you may answer, "But I was hungry, and ye gave me meat. I was thirsty, and ye gave me drink. I was a stranger (homesick and lonely), and ye took me into your home. I was naked, and ye clothed me. I was sick, and ye visited me. I was in prison, and ye came unto me." This kingdom is made of such as these. If we would use Christ's test of a Christian and separate the men-serving sheep from the do-nothing goats, there are not enough churches in this world to house the host of Christians, not even allowing for the church space that the goats would have to vacate.

It is pathetic to see how the world is struggling toward the Christian ideals almost in spite of the great institutions which have so long stood as the representatives of Christ. The pulpit no longer has a monopoly in proclaiming the truth. The truest religious life finds expression now in a thousand ways that have not yet been adopted by any institution.

Ten years ago Phillips Brooks said, "The great mass of men do not to-day belong in associated relations to the Christian Church." He shows that this

is because the Church has confined herself to the few partial phases of religious
activity she now displays, and is so
largely a mere conserver of dogma and
forms of worship.   This condition has
certainly not changed for the better since
1888, so far as the conventional church is
concerned.   There have been wonderful
strides along philanthropic and sociological lines which have enlisted thou-
sands of idle hands in service; and
institutional churches with walls as
broad as human activities are springing
up outside of the established channels.
"True religion is mightily stirring and
strenuously laboring in all these various
directions: and certainly if the Church
does not soon wake to an adequate sense
of her great privilege, facilities, and duty,
she will be left in the rear, instead of
being the leader of the universal movement toward better things."

For the Church this means that it loses
that great body of true and earnest men
who do not recognize their ideal of humanity in it.   But for many of these true
and earnest men, lovers of their fellows,

it means that they classify themselves as heretics and outcasts and unreligious. This in itself does not make them so except so far as a man unconsciously lives up to the reputation he makes for himself. Custom has so identified religion with its institutions in our minds that it is difficult to think of one without the other. It is a sign of vitality when a man inside of a church, or outside, recognizes his religion as his life independent of any means of expression. The commendation "well done" will give certain self-approval to any one who faithfully works with the trend of things, but it will come sooner if he knows he has a right to expect it. Many people come to know Christ by their righteous lives who would never know him through what often seems to them the fantastic and irrational processes of Christian institutions. Kindness and sympathy and mercy and love are eternal graces and know their kind wherever found, and are known by them.

But must I not believe this or that about God or Christ before I am reli-

gious? Most certainly not: only so much
as finds a response in your own life.   It
is only that part of God or Jesus that we
can appropriate, assimilate, and recognize
as possible and attainable in our own lives
that is of any use to us.

I have wished many times that religion
might be put upon a more natural and
commonplace basis; that so much of the
supernatural as is not founded on our
daily experiences or suggested by our
living might be removed.

The instinct of worship is indestructi-
ble in man's nature.

Religion is the activity of our sympathies, the feeding of our hopes, the
strengthening of our knowledge of the
trend of things.

"Men worship best together, but they
philosophize best alone."

But you say, "If I believe a part of
Jesus' life, must not I believe it all?"
No.   Your life is founded upon so much
of truth as you apprehend; the rest is
mystery to you, and whatever your attitude toward it, you do not keep it to
live with.

II.— LECTURE FRAGMENTS

My purpose in this course is, (1) to study the actual life of Jesus of Nazareth,—Christ as he was, not what men have thought he ought to be; (2) to study his words just as they were uttered and independent of commentaries and deductions, seeking to translate them into the terms of our life to-day; (3) to study the movement called Christianity, which, taking its name from its founder and its character from his principles, is without doubt the controlling force in our civilization to-day.

I recognize fully a certain limitation and embarrassment because the subject is so intimately connected with the religious life and thoughts of so many people. We dread to talk out loud about the things we associate with our churches

* Fragment of a lecture given at the beginning of the second semester in the course on the Life and Teachings of Christ.

and our prayers. We fear to bring into the glare of the sunlight those objects which seem so mysterious in the gloom of the cathedral. (Their healthy growth depends upon the amount of airing we give them.) Yet, in spite of these limitations, we will seek to study Christ and Christianity with our common senses, to test them by our human standards,— than which we, after all, have no other,— and to use them for our human and every-day necessities, which are the only ones that are real and important.

We will always worship, if we worship at all, that which is highest and truest *in* our lives. Nothing *outside* of our lives, however grand and noble, will ever be an object of worship.

We love to abstract ourselves from our bodies and our gods from our hearts and let the two flit off together into thin-aired heights where there is nothing to do because there is nothing to bother. But the God whom we serve and seek and pray to is concrete and anthropomorphic,— in us and not without us.

If Christ is an important factor in our

social life,—and he is without doubt the
most important,—why should we not
study him as we study Shakespeare, or
Luther, or Cæsar, and in exactly the same
spirit? If Christianity summarizes the
great forces which control and direct and
shape our civilization, why, then, should
we not study it as we would the French
Revolution, and in exactly the same
spirit?

In studying the person of Christ, his
biography and his character, we must do
it here in human terms. That is not saying that there are no other terms. But
the object of these lectures is to emphasize the humanity of Christ. There is a
theology of Christ; its study belongs to
metaphysics. There is a psychology of
Christ; its study belongs in its particular
place. Our study here is never distinct
from these two phases, but it is never
distinctly either. I shall endeavor to
exhibit the strong and pure, the successful, the virile nature, the picture of whose
life makes every true man stand taller
and every weak heart stronger.

It is a fact that no man can ever stand

true under the severest tests of life without increasing the self-respect of every other man who knows it. I never hear or see such instances without feeling proud that the human race can commit such virtue. So, setting aside all doctrines about Christ's nature and office, not for the reason that we do not hold them, but because they are not for us to study here, we will use this wonderfully simple and natural teacher's life as a key to solve the mysteries of our own lives.

A violet looking at the sun can know only its violet rays. Its knowledge fades on the one hand into actinic darkness; on the other, it is lost in the blues. Its knowledge of the great sun is limited by the work the sun has done in it, by its coincidence with the sun.

So with any ideal, with any friend. Friendship is but the common ground you and another occupy. Your best friend is he who widens this common ground and quickens your whole being, the one who makes you live the most. You do not measure your friendships by your brains, but by your pulse-beats.

Some of you say that you cannot reconcile your intellectual and your spiritual lives. I think you never will, if by *reconcile* you mean *coincide*. The head can never understand the heart, and the heart will always be doing such unreasonable things. But if the head is right in its sphere, it will find that the heart in its sphere is right also,— much harm may come from trying to identify them. Enter, then, into this study of Christ's life with your whole life, not your head only. You will satisfy me and my roll-book probably if you use your heads alone, but you yourself will be unsatisfied. In the clear light of Christ's teaching and life, study your own life, your appetites and ambitions, your social relations,— all your relations to God and to man. Apply to him the same tests that apply to your own life ; apply to yourself his standards of life. In this way only can we profitably deal with the facts of his life and the truths of his teaching. . . .

Christ talked in the language and figures of the every-day life of his time. To the people who listened he was not using the language of the temple, but of the street, of the field, of the lake-shore. He talked to be understood by people whom he understood. We can only comprehend his meaning by understanding the conditions of the time, the people, the figures of speech, the changes that have come to the words he used. . . .

The words of Christ were not religious in his day any more or less than a lecture in hygiene is to-day. We expect to hear them in church or connect them with religion, but they were not such words as his audiences were accustomed to hear in the synagogues. They have become so largely the ecclesiastical language of our time that it is hard for us to realize that they were not ecclesiastical then. "He taught not as the scribes taught." We can only get the meaning of these words by taking from them the ecclesiastical setting and expressing them in our own phraseology. . . .

MOST of us have a thought-world where we love to retreat and dream—a fair and happy land, where sweet fields are arrayed in living green and rivers with milk and honey flow, where this world as we know it is reproduced in fancy with all that is evil and uncomfortable and wearing left out. It is no larger than this world. It is no grander. It is not peopled by giants and heroes, but by men and women like ourselves, disembodied, we think, but just like ourselves in size, interests, attainments, loves, and hates, and differing from this only in the one particular, namely, that it is made of dreams, and contains only what seems attractive and desirable to us, while this is real, is worked in matter, and is full of restrictions and laws that hamper and limit. We call that our spiritual life, this our temporal; and because things

seem to run so smoothly there and so
roughly here, and especially because we
have to give so much of our time to this
and find it so hard to abstract ourselves
and dream of that, we argue that these
two are at war and it will be a grand day
when we are freed from this prison-house
and its hard labor. We argue so; and
yet we hardly believe it, for we have lots
of good times here, and when this ghostly
presence is not with us, reminding us
that this world is all a fleeting show, we
live this life to the full, and whenever
we forget ourselves we are often very
happy.

We have located most that we mean
by religion in that spiritual and unreal
world. The Bible, church service, prayer,
and much that we call *duty*, seems to be
reached down like a great good out of
that ethereal realm of mystery; and we
compel ourselves to do things without
reason, just because custom has connected
them with religion, and religion is spiritual, which often means also irrational.

We are told by preacher and teacher,
by friend and conscience, that we must

cultivate our spiritual natures, and so we
pore over our Bibles, hoping to absorb
spirituality.   We drop our tasks and try
to think of other things, to clothe our
fleshly bodies in figures of speech.   We
put ourselves in unnatural, unspontaneous
positions or activities and think they develop the supernatural and spiritual, and
then — we splash back into our native
element like a panting fish that has
leaped into the air to catch a sunbeam.
What is wrong?   If the spiritual life is
something taken out of this life of sense,
something I must prepare for by extra
exertions above and beyond those needed
to keep me alive and fed and clothed and
useful in this life of physical activity,
then the struggle is too hard for me.   I
cannot divide my energies.   I have not
time to stop living and go to church or
prayer-meeting, or to exercise my spiritual senses.   All such time is pilfered
from this life that I am leading, and I
will fall behind in the race if I permit
such waste.   Now, I am sure that one, if
not the only, reason church services or
prayer-meetings are not attended by

crowds, is because they have to do so largely with a theological and therefore unreal world. They supply no demand.

Many of us see no difference between this unreality and what we mean by spirituality. We abuse our own consciences and brand ourselves as heretics because we do not enjoy and find food in what we have been educated to believe is meat and drink for the spiritual life. If we examine the case with care, we will find that the trouble grows out of a misconception of the spiritual life. What, then, is the spiritual life?

In the first place, a spiritual life is activity — not dreaming. It is the refinement of this life — not for a moment or by a hair's-breadth now or ever separated from it. *It is this life*, if it is anything at all. It is wrong to speak of it as a separate life at all; it is this life, spiritualized. "It is the activity of the soul in its sensitiveness to the unseen world." But that unseen world is the world that expresses itself in the forms and forces and lives we see and handle and struggle with and help and hinder all about us.

It is that part of me that is not confined to my body, that part of me that leaps from my heart outward toward men and God and his world, not some dream of future happiness hidden in the inner chambers of my imagination to be realized when my disembodied spirit joins the favored circle inside the pearly gates. That is refined selfishness, and though it is called Heaven, it is gross materialism. Building our dream-castles out of pearls and gold and furnishing them with beds of ease is as harmful to character as if built like a sty and furnished with troughs. Let me illustrate: You and I have a common life — not our features, or stature, or appetites, or physical powers of any kind. These all vary infinitely, and, moreover, they are all things we cannot share. But we stand on common ground and exchange our thoughts; words fly back and forth, and they are not always empty. I talk to you, and so much of your life as is moved is mine, my dominion in you. I pick a thought from my heart and throw it into the air. Instantly a dozen of you

I

catch it; it is yours too; we are alike, we have that in common, we are to that extent attuned one with another. Now, nothing — *no thing* — passes from me to you. Yet one's whole life may be changed by such experiences. They are the cream of living. Within ourselves we may be struggling for possessions, for existence. Here is a " neutral ground " for barter. Widen the " neutral ground."

[Husband and wife. Completely united. Extend this to the world, to include all men. It can include all men. Sound men for it, and you always find it.] This is the life of the world, the common life, that will come and does come just in proportion as men make other people's lives their lives. I do not mean doing things for other people as outside of ourselves, for conscience' sake, or what not. That again is selfishness, though it is often called charity. But it does mean living a life common with other people, just as a mother makes the child's life her own, and as he will make hers his own when he is a man, joined to her, not by any material bands or physical cords,

but by a spiritual and a common love.
This is real charity, this is altruism, and
is possible only to that part of us that
dwells in the spiritual world, the only
part that we can have in common, even
with our best friend.

Now, this spiritual life is as wide as
the world. It develops as we add life
by life to our life, not only the lives that
are now on earth, but all who have left
messages to be read centuries after they
are gone. I read Emerson. Sentence
after sentence sets chords quivering in
my soul until I think and feel like Emerson—I am Emerson. I read words
spoken by Jesus. Again the throbbing
common life tells me we are one. I look
into the face of a friend. Soul meets
soul even before the tardy tongue can
speak and we share our common life.
So we find the world is a spirit-world,
and as we live on this common ground of
love and altruism more and more do we
know that the spiritual is developing in
us, that this life includes and swallows
up all other life.

More than this, we find men have

common aspirations, all upward. Their
ideals all face the same way—toward
the heavens. They are being led, perhaps
driven, in the same direction, and Nature
not always master, is more often father,
and speaks messages which the spirit of
man understands. A great world-spirit,
a universal life, is abroad, whispering the
same words to all men, leading men in
the same path, teaching the same laws of
righteousness, and brooding lovingly over
men to show them that they are one with
each other and one with it. Is not this
the Holy Spirit—God communing with
his children? Just as I share with you
my life, we together share his life.

Now, suppose your life is complete in
itself. You give all your time to your
studies—day after day adding to your
knowledge, studying machines, skeletons,
laws, perfecting your tools, not with any
one or for any one, but for yourself.
Blind to the messages that flash from
faces and from Nature, dead to the pulses
of power that throb around you, do you
not descend to the level of the machine
you study and cut off the common thing

that would link you with men and with God? You, then, have no spirituality.

Anything that you do for yourself, that centers in yourself, that is out of touch with the great world-life, is selfish; it is material, and it will never, can never, link you with the life of the world. Unselfishness, spirituality, usefulness, power of giving and receiving, come through sharing, and we can share only what is spiritual. If we really have this common life in us, and it is *life*, will we not enjoy and desire to exercise it together? And how shall we cultivate it? Is it not a very natural thing I have been speaking of? Just as I develop and cultivate any other power of my being, will I, by activity, by living, feed this life until it links me with all men and with God.

Religion belongs here. Identify her with her stuff, and she ceases to be religion. Religion is the activity of one's sympathies, the feeding of hope, the strengthening of one's knowledge of the trend of things on which we ground our faith. Formalism of any kind kills this life; spontaneity is necessary to its existence. Spontaneity is the overflow of a full life. Like all life, it is fed by exercise with its kind. The greater the freedom and the wider the range of one's activities, then, the larger will be one's hold on spiritual things. This explains Christ's constant warfare with the ritualism and rigid Temple system in his time, and the battle which must be fought with ecclesiasticism at all times.

When people come to believe that paying the expenses of a church is a chief part of religion, or uttering certain words is worship, or saying speeches in stated meetings is service, or doing anything for the sake of doing *it*, and not because it really expresses life, then the spiritual life disappears, and cold and formal and sterile is that which remains. . . .

. . . GOD, in the sense of Father, and all its derivatives, is not in the environment of the animal at all. Nor is my God in the environment of lower men. There is a God in their environment; they fear, they recognize sequences, but they have not risen into fellowship with him, nor detected personality. . . .

Growth is possible only by the putting away of old things, and old things are put away because new things are offered. It is not easy to put away old things — regeneration is not a painless process, and it is a continuous one. Fitness to live, socially or spiritually, is demonstarted only by sacrifice and breaking with the past.

We grasp some great thought to-day, and we must readjust our lives to it — rise into its level. Angels of light hold greater thoughts over our heads. We

135

can strive for them, and so grow taller,
or we can spend our time with what we
have, and after a while the angels will
stop coming.

When angel hands, at God's behest,
   Reach from the light o'erhead
The viands rare, from tables where
   The sons of God are fed,
The children grow, who strive to grasp;
   The Father's love is guiding.
And men grow tall who upward reach
   For that the clouds are hiding.

Nature is constantly putting a premium
on new things. . . . The worst enemy
of the better is the good. So if new
thoughts are thrown into your life which
show you something better than you ever
knew before, that which was best before
becomes wrong.

Christ at Nazareth made every man in
the village unchristian, whatever his life
may have been before. The pilgrims,
with their higher civilization, made it
impossible for Indians to live, as savages,
in North America. That Nature saw it
so, is proved by their disappearance.   A

knowledge of medicine and the laws of health makes it a crime to ignore this knowledge, and trust to charms or incantations. In other words, increase the environment of a man, and he must adapt himself to the wider life, or lose what he has.

But mere proximity — nearness of an object to an individual — does not mean that it is in his environment. An ignorant man may live in a great library, and learn nothing from it. A church in the slums is not necessarily among the influences that act upon the lives of the people there; it must first touch their lives.

God, to be in man's environment, must be reduced to human terms — incarnated. We must, if we would be helpers of men, get into their lives. We must talk to people, if we wish to get our message into their environment, in their own language. Ask a boy to be a Christian, and he may not know what you mean. Begin by asking him to be good to his mother, or kind to his sister, and when he has achieved these in a very small degree he will by them be lifted into higher possibilities. I sometimes wonder if we do well, in the pulpit, to hold up in so large a measure, ideal conditions of life. Would it not be wiser to take out of people's lives the best, and show how it may be made a little better?

I know a plucky little fellow who could hardly keep back the tears one day because he could not walk his big brother's stilts, but grew very happy walking some smaller ones made to fit him. And one day he came running with joy in his eyes, crying, "Oh, father, I can walk Harold's stilts!" Those high stilts had been in his environment all the time, but he had learned to walk them by walking his own.

I AM going to try to tell you what Christ meant by these words: "Ye must be born from above," and "partake of the kingdom of God." I shall talk very simply, because the subject is exceedingly profound, and we run great danger of leaving things we know and talking about things we imagine.

There is a *doctrine* of the new birth. Under many forms and names it is much talked about and wrangled over. Doctrines have to do with the causes of things and the how of things, and here where we have to do with facts alone we have nothing to do with doctrines about them. I shall speak of the *fact* of the birth from above. It is not a doctrine to be quarreled about, but an experience to be tested by any one who wishes to earn the right to talk about it.

In the first place, the kingdom of God

that Christ speaks of here is a figure, a
Jewish figure. Christ always means by
it the ideal order, when right and justice
and truth and purity will prevail here
among men, when the things we feel
ought to be will be, when man will
voluntarily do the things God is doing,
and the ideal conditions that we make
heaven of will really exist here on earth.
This kingdom of God really exists on
earth in a very small degree. In some
degree we have worked it into our pri-
vate lives and our social lives. Our
institutions and our practices are much
nearer the ideal than those of our fathers,
and this progress represents so much
growth toward the real presence of the
kingdom here. But it is so very, very
small, when we compare it with the
ideal state of affairs, that we have not
yet much cause for pride.

So the kingdom of God is something
that exists chiefly in our minds,—not
wholly, for some of it is incarnated in
men and women, and conditions and laws.
And in spite of our ignorance and weakness and perversity, we are working it

out of our minds into the real fabric of
life every day. But most of it is still
unreal, and exists in our minds, or is
drawn out as a working plan, very much
as an architect draws the structure and
makes a blue-print of it before he
begins to embody it in stone and wood.
It has a certain existence, and when a
man is helping place the stones and build
the structure according to the plans, its
reality grows on him daily, but we can
neither weigh it nor handle it. Its existence is spiritual. Not every man who
dresses the stones that are to form its
walls can comprehend the plans. They
are meaningless to the carrier of brick
or the mixer of mortar. Show them to
these lower minds, and they would find
them incomprehensible. I saw a hod-
carrier take up a blue-print and puzzle
over it sheepishly for a while, and then
put it down and go back to his mud-
mixing unenlightened. I was a little
nearer the architect in my culture, and
could see, from my higher ground, that
this child of the mind was going to be
worked out in brick and the very mortar

that that laborer was mixing. I had some knowledge that he had not, yet I had nothing to show for it that would serve as a means of making my understanding his.

Now, in much the same way we can detect the plans of the Being who is building his mind and will into our world.

We may see no more than the *stuff* we work with. We may think only in terms of matter and its laws, or we may rise into a very close fellowship with the Builder himself. And these purposes of his, these plans he is working out, are the kingdom of God that Christ speaks of. It is a spiritual kingdom, and while it may be *known*, yet its limits cannot be stated in terms of matter. This spiritual ideal kingdom is very real to some, while others are hardly conscious of its existence. Some live in it all the time, and neglect all other living, so that the spiritual work itself dies because it lacks the material it builds with. The mixer of mud is just as necessary to the master builder as the master is to the mixer of mud. And some who are faithfully and truthfully working on some of the parts never see themselves as a part of the great whole, and so lose the inspiration which comes to all who partake of the kingdom. When all is as it should be, the hod-carrier and the stone-cutter will dignify their labors by entering into the plans of the master.

Now, Christ says that if we would be partakers of this kingdom that is coming into the world we must be born from above. He means that a change in us must come which will enable us to see God's understanding of the things we do.

A child helps in some household task because it is told to do so. But after a while it catches some of its mother's spirit of unselfishness, and now it helps because it realizes that its life and the home life are one. Something new has come to it,—come from its higher mother-life. The child will develop this until it will be completely united with its mother. It has been born again from above.

Or to take the former illustration. Suppose a strike: the hod-carriers are out; the master builder away, perhaps misun-

derstood. Some friend of labor sits down
beside the hod-carrier, explains the plans,
and shows the purpose of the master,
shows how necessary co-operation is, in-
troduces master and laborer, so they can
talk over matters. The laborer sees things
in a new light. He is willing now to work
for the glory of it. He has caught the
spirit of the thing; the building is his.
He has been born again. He does not
cease to be a laborer. This new spiritual life is not a substitute for his other
life. It is added to it. He lives more
than he did before. This friend who
understood the heart of the builder and
the heart of the laborer has brought to
the hod-carrier new life which is more
abundant than the old. Now, some such
change as this must come to every one
who wishes to enter into any kind of a
sympathetic understanding of God's work.
His life is not a satisfied one until he
feels that the thing he is busy with is a
part of God's system and that he and all
good livers are working at the same thing.

When this comes a man is a member
of the kingdom and is born from above.

FAITH.

I WISH, at the outset, to secure your interest in this word.

It is not an attractive subject, for faith is made a mystery—a something intangible, which it is difficult for us to understand. It is supposed to be unrelated to natural causes—to be God-given, and bestowed on man for the asking. A lack of faith is often given as a reason for God's withholding it. It is urged upon all who would be religious, and is made a necessity upon which all blessings depend; yet, unlike all other necessities, it is difficult to acquire, and easy to lose.

Now, faith is a perfectly real thing—as real as religion. I wish to show as plainly as I am able, how important and vital it is to our religious lives. Many people who do not understand how they can have faith in God, when they have never tried him or tested him, will com-

prehend what I mean by faith in one's
self. I wish to show, first, that these
expressions mean the same.

Our ideals, our plans, our hopes all
lead us toward the unseen. Between us
and God, representing more than anything else the hold God has upon us, are
the dreams we hope to realize during
our university course. Our religious
lives are identified with these dreams.

Show me the things you hope for, and
I will write a definition of your God.
Some can see God only through their
own wishes and self-centered desires.
Others rise so far above themselves that
they seem to look back at the world
through God's eyes and to see what other
people want, and just where and how to
help. To me, our school life is religious.
Where one is pulling wires toward himself, a score are trying to make others
comfortable and happy. And the good
feeling which comes from this is really
God-feeling, and would not come unless
we had forgotten ourselves in the pursuit
of the ideal life where the interests are
common.

The pursuit of our ideals is a large part of our religion; it needs but the added element of worship to make it complete. And this will come when we recognize that these leadings toward better things—these ideals, these things we hope for—are, one and all, God touching us and manifesting himself to us.

When we can look our ideal in the face and say, "My Lord and my God," then we have become religious. The thing I most long for here, is to see that you each identify the good you find within—the best you recognize in your own lives—with the All-father without.

You will never really believe that God is your Father or recognize your own sonship, until you see that you want to do things as God does them, that goodness and truth mean just the same for you as they mean for him who rules all things. Then, like a very little child, you say, "Why, I am like my Father; I do things the way he does." No man can be of much use to the world until he can call the Creator—the great force back of

all things—Father. "Father" includes
the recognition of likeness, the identi-
fication of our ideals—the things we
hope for—with God. It includes the
implication of sonship. Do you remember when you reached up so far to take
hold of one finger of your father's hand,
and tried to step as far as he did, and
understood that you could grow like
him and do the things he did?

It is a great event in a boy's life when
he can say, "I and my father are one."
It is greater, when a man finds that he
can keep step with God; that he wants to
do, and can do, the things that God is
doing. But the term *father* includes one
thing more. It brings in the family feeling, that links our lives to the lives of
others and makes our interests common.
I have gloried in the development of a
child from the period where her interests were in her own affairs to that where
she cared for the things her brothers
needed. I have said, "We have another
member of the family, another partner."

So in the University life, when I see a
student interested in the lives of his fel-

lows, I know he has caught the spirit of the University, and that our great body is stronger by another member.

Now, there is an *esprit de corps* for the race. When a man feels the same kind of interest in his fellows that he feels in the members of his own household,— when he cares whether his brother is well housed, or well clothed, or well educated,— he has caught this racial *esprit de corps*, and feels toward the race just as God feels. For God is bringing it to pass that all men shall be well cared-for. You can judge of your faith, therefore, and define it, by studying your own attitude toward these great questions—God, and self, and man.

Faith is the hold you have on the ideal, the distinctness of your vision of these relationships. It is the evidence you have that your plans and desires and hopes will be realized. You surely would not give much time to service of God or of fellows unless you believed it would pay. If you believe that you and God are alike and one, it is because your life is proving it to you. If you look ahead

into the future, and see how you can be
of some use, and make something of
yourself, and become like the dream of
the father there is within you, and if you
are willing to work here four years to
realize your dream, your hope is founded
upon some real evidence that things will
go your way. That evidence is your
faith. It represents what you are, and
connects your past with your future.

When men search with so much heart-
ache for faith in order that they may
believe, they think they are groping in
the darkness to find God. They think if
they can only find him, they will get
faith from him. It is not faith in God
that they need, but faith in themselves.
They know God will do his part. They
have perfect confidence that he will run
the universe all right. It is self-confi-
dence that men need, belief that they can
do their part. No man ever falls away
from God and loses confidence in him
until he has first warped and twisted his
life by falling away from himself. In
other words, faith does not depend upon
anything God does or may do, in answer

to our prayers, but upon us,--upon our training, our experience, our knowledge.

The University has much to give us; our power to take depends upon ourselves. Heaven will not supply the lacking of a lazy life. It is full of blessings for those who seek them,—great armfuls waiting for great arms to reach them. Puny, untrained arms can carry only little loads, and Heaven is not responsible for untrained arms. People who expect to receive much, must be prepared to receive much. If you go to the well with a little bucket, you must expect to draw only a little water.

As the will is the man willing, so belief is the man believing. A man in the full possession of all his powers is a man of faith.

And yet men confess lack of faith with so little shame! They are content to act like babes in religious matters. They would not dare confess that they were ignorant, would not speak above a whisper, if they told you that they were bankrupt, but yet exhibit a kind of pious, though melancholy, pride in telling you that they are religious fizzles. As if God were responsible! Just so, an habitual loafer will always blame the Government if he is out of work.

The danger that some fear from socialism and kindred movements, will never come from those who vote their convictions. They are patriots; forgetting themselves, remembering their country. The danger will come from those who blame the Government for their own failures and seek to vote the accumulations of industry into the hands of idleness. They are parasites, not patriots, who cling to new movements, misrepresenting them, and misusing them for selfish ends. And so with the Church. She must go before the world with a load of weaklings who importune Heaven for that which they should themselves supply. They think that keeping themselves humble and inefficient is "being like little children," and have not yet learned the truth that the power of a church depends upon the character of its men and women just as much as the power of a banking-house depends upon the integrity of its employees.

Here are two views of faith: A little girl once woke from an unpleasant dream, left her bed, and passed out into the hall calling to her father. He stepped into the hall below, and seeing above him the little sunny-haired, white-robed figure, thought to test her confidence in him. Reaching out his arms to her, he said, "Jump, Gertie," and without an instant's hesitation, she jumped into the darkness and was safe in her father's arms. This was not faith, but inexperience; she believed in her father, not in herself.

To me there is no better example of faith than in the words of the Psalmist, who had tested God through a long life: "I have been young, and now am I old; yet have I not seen the righteous forsaken, nor his seed begging bread." Or the twenty-third Psalm: "Yea, though I walk through the valley of the shadow of death, I will fear no evil; for thou art with me; thy rod and thy staff they comfort me. Surely goodness and mercy shall follow me all the days of my life."

So I make this assertion, that faith — faith in self, faith that puts God to the test, faith that links God and man, and is the key to all the riches of heaven — is the result of experience, and is to be won like any other power, by persistent and constant exercise. You, and you alone, hold the key to your heaven.

I will try to show how this is true. Carlyle says, "Hope is the great constant in a man's life." We live not for what we have, but for what we want — hope for. "This is a great truth; it uncovers the divine part of us. To live with only a recognition of our present possibilities, to draw all our joy and comfort from such things as we can now get under our touch and sight, as so many are telling us, — this, I conceive to be thoroughly brutish. It makes man but another bird among the trees, or another insect humming in the evening air. But to hope and wait for the highest and best we can conceive, — this expands life, and makes it as large as infinity. This affords a field for the solution of its mysteries, for the cure of its ills, for regaining some of the lost things, for realizing the complete union with God for which man always strives."

But how do we know that these enchanting dreams will ever be realized? It is easy to build air-castles, another thing to believe they will become real.

Is there any evidence for these things we hope for? First, examine the future. It is dark. We peer into its formless void, and tremble before its emptiness. We call God, and hear the taunting echoes of our own despair. Hope is not a bird of night that pushes across that dark gulf, and expects us to follow. Hope is one of the three things that abide with us. We get nothing from the future; let us look behind. There much becomes clear. Some of us have been a long time with the past, and have learned to see God in it. Life has been a period of testing. We have been tested, and we have tested God. He has never failed. We have never found him anywhere but at our sides. We have sought him, in

the heaven away from our life, and have
cried many times, like Philip, "Show us
the Father."

But we have always found him in some
incarnation who stands by our side, or
rests in our hearts. As we have failed,
we find that our confidence, our belief in
self and in our future, is shaken. We
hope for much, but do not have the evidence that makes its coming certain. As
we have stood unflinching, and have quit
ourselves like men, we have come to believe in ourselves, and have acquired a
strong confidence in regard to the future.
We have abundant evidence from the
past—we have grown a man of belief
within us. So, when the future asks its
questions, we look within and find the
answer there. So we acquire the power
of walking without fear or question into
the future, because the past has made us
believers. And our belief, our faith, is
the evidence that the things we hope for
shall come to pass. We are daily making our past—laying the foundation for
hope. 'If we daily walk with God, the
future will be full of God.'

But some one says, "This puts the whole responsibility of my religious life and my future life upon me." That is just where it ought to be. Instead of putting ourselves in the attitude of pensioners on God's bounty, let us be what all true children are — partners and co-laborers.

The weakest can be stronger if he will, and as we acquire belief in ourselves doubts will vanish. Faith is the momentum of a life of righteousness; the distance into the future a life can run that has been running right in the past.

An iron-foundry, a flour-mill, a brick-kiln derive their names and their characters not from the rough material they receive, but from the articles they give out. It is so with men. We measure them not by their accumulations or their knowledge; they are just what they give out to us.

Character seems to be made, more by the "output" of our lives than by the "intake." It is well to learn; it is better to teach. It is well to receive; it is better to give. Often we overlook this, and when we find ourselves suffering from spiritual ennui or disordered religiously, we rush to some soothing-syrup. That brings artificial feeling of comfort and ease, but fails to attack the disease at its very roots.

For it is a disease. I have no good name for it, but it is common. There

are many people who can eat great
hearty meals and do nothing whatever
with them, unless sitting with kindred
spirits magnifying gnats until they are
as big as elephants, or mole-hills until
they swell mountain high, is doing something.

Or sometimes the disease passes
through another phase and affects the
brain. Great thoughts, abstracted from
life by master hands, are taken in until
the gorged intellect, confused and dazed,
sees visions and dreams dreams that life
can never realize, and that unfit the unhappy victim for social fellowship with
those who toil and bear burdens.

We hear. We store our minds and
note-books with rules and maxims. We
know *how* to live. But this is not life.
When our knowledge becomes motive,
and only as it becomes motive, does it
pay us for its getting. Only that part of
our knowledge or our conviction which
becomes action solidifies into character.
All the rest is like the sand, blown by
the winds, - mountain-high at times, but
fleeting.

There is a class, and many of us belong to it, that is especially tempted to lead an unnatural life. All of us have to give a certain portion of our time to living, to bread and butter and clothes and taking care of our bodies. During that time we are safe. We are working for what we receive. That is always perfectly safe. It is of the remaining time that I speak —the time you have left after this necessary work is done, your spare time,— that is, over and above what you give to maintain your body. This time is beset with danger. It is so easy to become a recipient, to read good things and listen to good things. It is really hard to become a giver. We have to compel ourselves. Our natural laziness, fed by this atmosphere of laziness, would keep us lolling about the easy chairs all day long, did we not *drive* ourselves into exercise.

And there is a certain kind of apathy —fed by lecture courses, sometimes— that makes it easy for us to keep our best thoughts to ourselves, and hard for us to hunt up some fellow and give them to him.

When we overeat at the table our obliging and much-abused stomachs take care of the material as long as they can, work it over, pass it into the system until all the store-chambers are full; then our heads get to aching, and our eyes are blurred, and blue devils keep us company, and we cannot see things clearly. So some analogous symptoms are always found in those who hear and do not *do*. The disordered mind begins to doubt and fear, and sees strange visions of esoteric unrealities and grotesque philosophies. And theories that never can be lived cloud the life.

Our doubts and fears and vagaries will vanish when we begin living again ---just as clouded eyes and dull aches will disappear when we take a day's outing.

I need not further emphasize the call to work. Surely 1 have done that in these lectures. I have tried to show that it is laid upon every living thing, and upon every part of every living thing —necessary to our very existence. It is more important that men should be given something to do than something to

K

eat. We learn far more through activity than through meditation or reading or listening to sermons or lectures.

Some of you have wished that these words of mine were printed that you might read them over and talk them over. I should rather fear the result. The only good that can come to any of you through these lectures is to forget the words and put into action the emotion. If you have been changed, the change is the important thing. Let the words go.

Now, I wish to show you that in the "Kingdom" work is the primary thing, activity is the essential thing. *Pay*—that is of secondary importance. How many people waste their lives working for pay, instead of working for work. Was it Lessing who said, "If God should put in one hand all truth and in the other the search for truth, I would throw away the truth, and spend eternity in the search"?

We carry our misconception into the religious life, and make sensation and emotion the *end* of religious activity.

We perform tasks in order that we may *feel* good. We praise that meeting that arouses our emotions, as if a man or woman had no other reason for being than to feel good. Religious enjoyment, like every other enjoyment, is only incidental. Many try, and succeed too, in purchasing *feeling* by working for it. They exchange services or rituals for emotion just as they would give money for a narcotic — so much sensation for so many pennies.

The church is not a mere club to promote enjoyment; nor is its work primarily to promote the devotion and worship of its members. The church is to disciple all nations, reform all society, enlighten all moral darkness, alleviate all distress. Let it do that work, and it cannot escape emotion and increased devotion. Take hold and help, and you will have more emotion than you know what to do with. To try to be religious while neglecting urgent duty is to begin at the wrong end. Religion must be thoroughly mixed with usefulness to keep it wholesome.

There are two views of life. We may choose either.

One is to ask, "How much am I worth? What have I done? How much will my services purchase me? What can I get out of the world?" The other is to ask, "What am I? How much can I give? How much can I do?" Work is the means—the end is man. Enjoyment or position are incidental accompaniments that always come when you work a man.

The man who works for pay is not the best worker. A teacher whose object in teaching is to draw a salary is not capable of imparting to his pupils what they need. But if he enters earnestly into his task and teaches for the sake of teaching, he forgets the pay, and excels in his work. This truth holds in religion. He who does good because it pays may not be good, but he who is good does good without thought of reward.

Bargaining prevents being. The man who goes through life thinking only of the heaven at the end of it, is apt to experience many of the tortures of hell

on his journey. It is hard enough to
lay by money. It is far harder to lay by
character and good deeds with which
to purchase eternal life. The young
man who came to Jesus and asked,
"What good thing shall I do that I may
have eternal life?" had spent his life
accumulating virtues, but had forgotten
to *be*.

We look to heaven for the mysterious
wedding garment, and hope that it may
fit us when we put it on. We overlook
the fact that it is being formed now in
our very tissues, fitting us as closely as
our habits, and more nearly like us than
our shadows.

"Long, long ago there lived a saint so
good that the astonished angels came
down from heaven to see how a mortal
could be so godly. He simply went
about his daily life, diffusing virtue as
the star diffuses light, and the flower
perfume, without even being aware of
it. Two words summed up his day: he
gave, he forgave. Yet these words never
fell from his lips; they were expressed

in his ready smile, in his kindness, for-
bearance, and charity.

"The angels said to God, 'O Lord,
grant him the gift of miracles!' God
replied, 'I consent; ask him what he
wishes.'

"So they said to the saint, 'Should
you like the touch of your hands to heal
the sick?' 'No,' answered the saint; 'I
would rather God should do that.'
'Should you like to convert guilty souls,
and bring back wandering hearts to the
right path?' 'No; that is the mission
of angels.   I pray I do not convert.'
'Should you like to become a model of
patience, attracting men by the luster of
your virtues and thus glorifying God?'
'No,' replied the saint; 'if men should
be attached to me, they would become
estranged from God.   The Lord has
other   means   of   glorifying   himself.'
'What do you desire then?' cried the
angels.   'What can I wish for?' asked
the saint, smiling.   'That God gives me
his grace; with that shall I not have
everything?'

"But the angels insisted, 'You must

ask for a miracle, or one will be forced upon you.' 'Very well,' said the saint; 'that I may do a great deal of good without ever knowing it!'

"The angels were greatly perplexed. They took counsel together, and resolved upon the following plan: Every time the saint's shadow should fall behind him or at either side, so that he could not see it, it should have the power to cure disease, soothe pain, and comfort sorrow.

"And so it came to pass. When the saint walked along, his shadow, thrown on the ground on either side or behind him, made arid paths green, caused withered plants to bloom, gave clear water to dried-up brooks, fresh color to pale little children, and joy to unhappy mothers.

" But the saint simply went about his daily life, diffusing virtue as the star diffuses light, and the flower perfume, without ever being aware of it. And the people, respecting his humility, followed him silently, never speaking to him about his miracles. Little by little, they even came to forget his name, and called him only 'The Holy Shadow.'"

So the power of the helper lies first in his power of becoming unconscious, of forgetting himself and any reward, and losing himself in his work. And this faculty for losing one's self in work can come only by practice. Begin to carry other people's burdens, and look for trials and chances to help; you will be awkward at first, as when you first rode a wheel, but you will soon become expert and unconscious. And if you ever have time to examine yourself for feeling, you will find you are wonderfully happy.

"But what can I do?" so many ask. They look for some great thing. Big sacrifices are easier than little ones. You probably are not fit for a great work, or you would be doing it. But you are working in the truest sense when you identify the lives of others with your own. And I mean the whole life. We narrow the conception of religious work, and make it mean teaching a Sunday-

school class, or visiting the poor and the
prisons.   Do you know that some of the
Lord's poor sit in palaces with their
hands chained by luxury, and so imprisoned by social customs that the God
in them is dying? And you, if you touch
them at all, might take the poor sick
divinity out walking for a while. A new
thought will do it—a breath of the fresh
air of life.

Anything whatever that widens the
horizon of a man, that makes two rush-
lights burn where but one burned before,
that sweetens a moment of life, the least
drop you take from the bitterness that
fills so many lives—this is religious
work. Do it with your might. But be
tactful. It requires endless tact to help.
No one can be a helper and not think
and plan and contrive. It costs to sympathize, for true, helpful sympathy means
literally feeling just as others do—a
sensible participation in their joy or
woe. And we cannot become real helpers until we sympathize. Look for the
fruits of your work not in what you do,
nor in what you give. A large share of

these will always be hidden.   Look into
your heart.   Measure your work by your
life.

For God withholds the harvest store
  From hands that cast the seed,
And hides the golden treasures in
  The heart that felt the need.

We never know how many fold
  The grain has multiplied;
How many little mouths have fed,
  How much has failed or died.

But we may know the wealth and joy
  That spring from freely giving;
The gladdest, maddest joys of life
  Are those that come from living.

Count not your garnered treasures o'er,
  They are but seed for sowing;
Throw them broadcast into the world,
  And know the joy of growing.

Toil not to increase your stores,
  God's gifts exceed your suing,
But toil that ye may Godlike be,—
  Being is born of doing.

SERVICE.

It is a mistake common to us all to think that looking at pleasing aspects of the truth, subjecting ourselves to sensations, hearing good things about things, is adding to our power and developing our character.

Sensations are within the reach of all. Preachers deal in them sometimes. Our rituals and our choirs give them. There are books that pile up great waves of emotion in us almost as real as if we had earned them. I have read of battles that were so vividly portrayed that my cold blood grew hot and I felt like a hero; but I cooled down, a little more weary than before,—that was all. I have listened to great preachers who talked so familiarly of holy things and made them so real that earth has seemed dreary when I touched it again. Emotions are dangerous things unless they find an outlet in action. We can so narcotize ourselves with holy things that our senses will lie to us.   We can read these sayings of the Master until we can feel like Christians. We can, as the Buddhist urges, meditate on holy things until we feel as though we were holy too.   But periods of rude awakening come.   We find we have been hearing and not doing, saying Lord! Lord! and not doing God's will.

I would not appear to condemn our emotions, but to show how little they mean,— nay, how they are even harmful, if we do not work them off in service. So large a part of our religion is emotional that we are apt to think this is all there is of religion.   We cry, "Could we but stand where Moses stood," wishing we might live all the year round in the Holy of Holies instead of once a year.

> I would not live where men are not,
>   But turn from Holiest Place
> To let the lower brother see
>   The glory in my face.
>
> Nor could I dwell on Sinai's top
>   Alone with God most high;
> I must love him whose lower lot
>   Knows less of God than I.

Religion has in it two elements—receiving and giving. We are in danger of thinking too much of what God can give us, of what our church is to us, of how we can change our lives and build our characters. This is the only way not to receive.

Exercise the angel; do not try to exorcise the devil. No animal lives for itself, or is allowed to live for itself. Nature executes drones. Until a man has learned to give and to train himself for giving, to work for others, to plan and study for others, to live for others and spend himself for others, and save nothing for himself, nature exacts pound after pound of flesh until only enough remains to make a fossil. Men groan over a tenth. The God of nature exacts all. Our nature exacts all. "Use it, or lose it." All your learning, achievement, discovery, your good times, your blessed experiences have not found the reason for their existence until you touch the heart of humanity. Our hands may lose all we give—our hearts lose nothing.

SYMPATHY.

EVERYWHERE to-day the cry of the suffering is not, "Oh, for somebody to pity me!" but, "If only somebody could understand!"

Sympathy is what the world needs rather than pity. Sympathy requires a free use of the imagination, to comprehend the experience and condition of another. People long more than anything else to be understood. "Put yourself in his place" is old advice, and it fits most of the relations of life. It measures the power of the speaker over his audience, the politician over his party, the preacher over the pew, the teacher over his students, and your power over those you would help.

Putting yourself in his place is sympathy,— nothing else can be. And if you are planning for dominion over men in any way, your dominion will be measured

by your understanding of them. The
fisherman who understands things from
the standpoint of the trout, is the one
who comes home with a full basket. The
teacher who talks from the student's
standpoint, is the good teacher. The
friend who can put himself in your
place, is the friend you love most. And
so it goes. To be sure, this kind of sympathy costs. People in trouble do not
want you to say, "Poor thing!"—any
one can say that. A student talking over
a burden heavier than most students
bear, offered me no way of helping.
"What can I do?" I asked. "Nothing;
I knew you would understand," was the
answer. Since I have learned that my
power to help people rests entirely on
my ability to see things from their standpoint, I have been very glad for some of
my deepest losses, because they have ex-
plained the losses of others to me.

But you are not going to be able to
help men without weighting yourself with
their burdens. This is what sympathy
means—suffering with those who suffer.
You will have an easier time if you do

not take my advice in this matter. Do not cultivate your sympathetic nature, and none of the pains or troubles of life will come to you except your own. But it is also true that a thousand joys and the riches of noble natures will be unknown to you.

Sympathy is our *touch* with our fellows; and we are made by our fellows far more than we realize, far more than by any other influence whatever. So, as a part of your training for life, I urge you to cultivate and develop your sympathies.

"Follow me, and I will make you fishers of men," is a call to service,—not a call to be religious only, but to toil, labor, love. And it involves sacrifice. One mark of the authenticity of any call is not so much, will it pay? as will it cost? "If you do not buy the world with your blood, you will never buy it."

PRAYER.

PRAYER is the heart of religion. I recognize the fact that there are dangers attending the discussion of this subject, and I hope not to arouse doubts in your minds. By reaching a better understanding of the nature of prayer, we may perhaps remove some of the difficulties.

This is an age of questioning, and we are all apt to mislead ourselves, to think that our little back yards are God's universe. If we work with matter, we overlook spirit. If we dwell much apart with spiritual things, we are prone to deny matter. Now, I believe that perfect harmony and rest can be found only when these two realms are equally represented in our lives.

The question is often asked, "Does not science make prayer impossible?" or, "Does not evolution destroy prayer?" Yes; it does destroy a certain kind of prayer. For those whose God is away outside of this world, whose prayer is a sort of beggary, who have not yet risen into the conception of Fatherhood and sonship, who do not participate in the divine life of the world, but hold themselves off to one side as spectators and aliens,— for all such, science does destroy prayer. It ought to.

But real prayer is not beggary; it is communion. That is, two beings who have the same natures and desires and language get on common ground. That is communion, and that is prayer.

Our idea of prayer is intimately connected with our idea of God. God adapts himself to men. Many pray, "Thy will be done" who really mean, "My will be done." It is strange, marvelous, how this, the holiest and at the same time the most powerful agent within man's reach, is degraded by selfishness until it becomes the means of separating those whom it should join.

We build our homes, and fill them with our idols, and surround them with our desires, and then cry to God, "Here is

my life; these are my precious things;
take care of them, and I will bless thee;
grant my desire, and I will extol thee."

And then when we are led out into a
larger life, and have to leave some of our
choicest treasures behind, we cry aloud,
"O Lord, where art thou? Why hast
thou forsaken me?" It often takes a
long life to realize that God may desert
our *stuff*, that he may refuse to live in
our air-castle, but that he never deserts
us. The first view of the relation between God and man is the child's view..
All centers in self. The love-light in
the mother's eyes shines but to bless;
the child asks and expects everything.
After a while, when he has risen into
the realm of fellowship, he and his
mother talk over the things that are best
for both of them.

Man can conform to God's will when
he grasps the great idea that he is the
child of God, being made in his image,
having his very nature, and capable of
infinite growth toward him. Then he
understands that his chief business in
life is to find God's will and do it. When

he realizes that his whole life is wrapped up in God, that he can exist only as he conforms to God's will, that he can succeed in nothing that is contrary, and in everything that is parallel, to that will, then his prayer is not "Give me my way," but "Thy will be done."

God's definition of righteousness and man's are the same. What is true and right and best for God is also true and right and best for man. Man may not have risen very far toward God's conception of these things, but far enough to know that right, so far as he knows it, is right.

God's superior knowledge, combined with his righteousness, makes him immutable. I mean he is perfectly consistent with himself, unchangeable; constant as sunshine, but constantly good; almost forcing us by penalties and warnings to choose the good. This is the God of science, and of the Bible, and of experience, though not always of theology. Do we not see his counterpart in a wise father who knows when to say Yes, and how to say No, and always says what is best; not yielding to teasing,—withholding even when it hurts,—yet giving all that is needed, and many things that are not prayed for?

In times of great stress it is natural that man should cry for special things; but we must never forget, when we think God is forsaking us, that such a thing is an impossibility. Our very conception and definition of man includes the God in his environment. "The hope of the future lies in the realization by individuals that none are ever for a moment forsaken by God; that the ministry of his spirit is constant, impartial, pervasive, and never-failing."

But I hear some asking, "What is the use of prayer? If God will not give what we want unless it is best for us, if he will give what we need whether we ask it or not, why not sit back and stoically take life as it comes?" I hope I have suggested the answer in previous lectures, where I have endeavored to show how far man may grow, and how large a part he has in his own development. The object of prayer is the union

of God and man, and this is possible in
two ways: by changing the will of God,
or by modifying the will of man. The
Father may go to the prodigal and, if we
can imagine such a thing, live on husks
with him, and help him feed swine, or
the son may go to the Father and change
his life to adapt it to the life of the
Father. "The essential element of prayer
is to bring two things into unison, the will
of God and the will of man. Superstition imagined, no doubt, that prayer
would change the will of God; but the
more spiritually minded have always
understood that the will which must be
modified, was the will of man."

I do not believe that real prayer is
ever wasted. No man who has talked
with God, whatever God's message to
him may be, whether he has granted or
denied that man's requests, can ever come
back to the same level of existence. He
is a little higher, a little nearer his
Father, for that communion.

The elements of prayer are these:
God's will, man's will, "I will." The
first represents a knowledge of all things

good and evil; the second represents a choice of some things by the finite one; and the third represents man's obedience to God.

Let us consider some objections to this view of prayer. One asks, "Cannot God overrule his own laws?" Why should he, if those laws express his nature? "If God should wink at a single act of injustice, the universe would fall to pieces."

And another argues, "If God's laws are immutable, then men are not free; they are driven whether they would or not." This is fatalism; and to such a one I would answer, we are free under gravitation or any law of physics or chemistry, yet we cannot change those laws.

And yet another exclaims, "But God is unapproachable. I cannot understand how prayer can be of any use. Every individual is apparently under inflexible laws, and is, in the end, what heredity and environment make him." That is true; but so far from making the case desperate, I am going to show that in that very fact just stated lies the foundation

of our assurance. Man is the product
largely of heredity and environment, but
God is in the environment. A man said
recently, "I do not believe in prayer or
churches, but I never get off on the ocean
without experiencing a kind of uplift
that leaves me a better man." Now, by
"uplift" he did not mean seasickness,—
he was an old sailor. He meant, though
he did not say it, that God's spirit and
his spirit came together and held communion. God is in our environment, and
will be more and more so as we grow
and pray.

"Oh, that the scales from our blind eyes
    Would fall, and let us see
The Father's hand on rock or cliff,
    On bird or flower or tree!
Oh, that our deadened ears might hear
    The Omnipresent One
Whose pulse-beat echoes in our hearts
    When we are most alone!"

Let me ask again, What constitutes
human environment? Nature is a part
of it; also men both in their corporate
and spiritual relations. And, beside

these, there is an environment of spirit, which we call God.

The influences that mold men are not all material. Society is not made up of a lot of physical bodies. "Not bodies, but spirits, constitute the social environment. The Christian doctrine of the Holy Spirit means not only that each man is surrounded by human spirits, but also that his days are passed in the presence of the absolute, the Universal Spirit immanent in the universe."

Now, it is just as surely true that the spirit of man can commune with God, and learn his will, as it is true that friend can commune with friend. And this communion is prayer. It is only as we are materialists that we fail to understand prayer. As we rise into the spiritual realm, prayer becomes a reality. And there is an active element in prayer. It is itself the chief agency by which God answers prayer. It is not an emotion alone. Prayer which does not lead to action is unworthy the name. Prayer is an activity of the whole being. We answer many of our own prayers.

How lightly we play with eternal things sometimes! In our religious talk great big words are emptied of their infinite significance and thrown back and forth as lightly as tennis-balls. We talk of heaven as glibly as if it were in the next county, and describe the inner workings of the heart of the Eternal as though it were our own. As we grow wiser, we talk less, and our words grow heavy with thought. There is one word I wish to load with heavier meaning. . . .

We perhaps have, each one of us, a meaning for rest. I, of course, do not mean to discuss here the various devices for doing nothing. Men work harder sometimes doing nothing than in the performance of a task. But by rest I mean freedom from care and worry, from fear that things are not going right — chafing and fretting, worries great and small.

186

Would it not be a grand thing to be rid of all of these? We think it would, though, as I shall show, many of us have really a good time with our woes, and would be at a great loss to know what to talk about if we did not have them. Note the melancholy strain running through our talk sometimes; and in our hymnals we find such words as these:—

"Oh, where shall rest be found,
    Rest for the weary soul?
'T were vain the ocean-depths to sound,
    Or pierce to either pole.

" The world can never give
    The bliss for which we sigh;
'T is not the whole of life to live,
    Nor all of death to die.

" Beyond this vale of tears
    There is a life above,
Unmeasured by the flight of years;
    And all that life is love."

Is the world a vile world? Is the body a leprous thing to which man is chained? I love it, especially when I have mastered it. Is life a long night-

mare, of which it is a crime to rid ourselves, and a blessing to be rid of? I
love life. There is so much more sweet
than bitter for those that look for nectar.
I have great affection for my body,
troublesome as it sometimes is. We
have gone through so much together,
that we are used to each other, and I
really like to gratify it and treat it fairly
well. And the world, the dear old world,
has so many more angels than devils in
it, and grows such rare flowers of prom-
ise on its grave-mold, that I would not
trade places with the greatest archangel.

Why, then, is this melancholy wail so
prominent in religious conversation and
literature? Is it true that faith and hope
do not abide, while pain and sorrow do?
The answer is complex. Men love, in a
a certain way, gloom and melancholy.
Weeds of mourning give a peculiar comfort, and the hideous side of life appeals
to a part of our nature. Men love mystery, and cling with marvelous conserv-
atism to superstitions long after their
intellectual powers have outgrown them.
The modern quack or miracle-worker

finds followers everywhere. It is a fact as strange as it is paradoxical, that progress toward brighter light and wider liberty has always been accomplished in spite of the inertia and opposition of the great mass of people who have stoned their prophets and crucified their Messiahs chiefly because they were disturbers and turned the world upside down.

Men love ease and rest. Their busiest moments are when, like ants, they rush frantically about to settle their disturbed nests. Will man evolve himself? Was Godlikeness wrapped up in some primeval savage, and has it gradually and easily unrolled itself until a Godlike man is the result? No. If human history shows progress, it is not to man's credit. Man has been a fighter all his life, and not a willing one; he has fought for peace and ease, but has never found them. Instead, power has come to him. Enlarged borders mean heavier responsibilities—new burdens for empty shoulders.

Left alone, man would never progress. His body would become the slave of habit, his mind an encyclopedia, his religion a dead skeleton of theology, wired by some creed or system of morality. The world-movement which we identify with the name of Christ is not an up-swelling of the life of humanity. The tides are caused by external forces. "Whatever amount of power an organism expends is the correlate and equivalent of a power that is taken into it from without."

The leaven of Christ is working throughout the world; it has become a part of man's environment, and there is no rest for man until he has conformed to this environment and measured up to the standard of Christ. It is evident, then, that the rest of having nothing to do will never come in this life, or in any other. If we are to look for happiness, it must be of another kind.

In contradiction to Montgomery's hymn, "Oh, where shall rest be found?" I affirm that rest,—that is, absence of worry, and wear, and weariness,— recuperating, invigorating, and bringing content,— can be found here, in this world, in this body, and during this life. This world withholds bliss from those only who sigh. It is a vale of tears for those only who will not look for the rainbow tints reflected from the falling drops.

The old view of life was a vicious one. It directed man away from the only source of happiness and peace, made his standards external, forced upon him commandments and creeds, made his religion a life of hard service and restriction, made character seem like a library or a collection of curiosities — an accumulation of virtues. It withdrew men from the only field where character could be won. It destroyed man's faith in himself. He was guided by authority and ruled by precedent. There are many who want conduct decided for them, who want a prop to lean on; to them such a religion would appeal, and for them such a religion means moral destruction. This has been the great error of the Roman Catholic Church: she does not have faith in men.

It set men to watching their own conduct and studying themselves, enumerating their virtues, and selfishly parading their ills. Spontaneity was destroyed by it, and there is no happiness where spontaneity is lacking. It made happiness an end, and caused men to "take thought" for life.

Happiness, which means peace, rest, contentment, is not something to be worked for; it comes only as one of the results of living. Make it the goal of your life, and you never reach it. Forget it—live!—and lo! happiness is by your side, your most efficient helper. The peace of God is the peace of living and growing.

Externalism—placing all our dependence upon rules, precedent, creeds, and doctrines—this brings unrest and worry. We fear when these seem to fail. The greatest sin is not ignorance, but laziness; not in not knowing what to do, but in not doing what we know. Happy is that man who has within himself all that is necessary for life.

These words of Christ,—"The kingdom of God is within you,"— were momentous words. He did not say the kingdom of God is to be found in heaven by those who can get through this vile world. It is not to be found in any organization whose rigid walls separate sheep and goats, nor in any system of rules or belief by which a faltering hand can steer through life when judgment wavers. It does not come to us through any possession; the rarest jewels lose their charm when once possessed. Nor is it to be found in pomp, or power, or ambitions realized—in accumulations that permit gratification and ease. Care-worn faces and aching hearts are linked with these. Kingdoms built on these have crumbled, and no human institution has yet been able to withstand the mighty power of those seven words.

How can I have the kingdom within me? By drawing to myself the choicest things of the world? Beholding its beautiful pictures, reading its wisest books, singing its glorious songs? By erecting in my heart a shrine to each of the gods, or enthroning there Jehovah himself? By defining right, by decrying wrong? By ruling myself with a rod of

M

iron, and removing myself from temptation and trial in a life of asceticism? No. My little life is soon filled, and grows morbid from overcrowding when I seek to accumulate. And when I seek to build a secret altar to a god in my heart, I find it some caricature of self I have seated there. And rules for living are tiresome things that keep me asking, "What lack I yet?" The kingdom is not like these.

I saw one day a mountain spring come bubbling up among the pebbles and sand. As it piled up the water, it was gurgling like a child, and sparkling. Its stream flowed down the mountain-side, bathing the roots of ferns and trees. The birds drank, and thanked God; the herds and the tired laborers satisfied their thirst. Away on the mountain the spring knew nothing of its overflow. It took what came, and eagerly passed it on. It lived and was happy.

"Man in his inmost being is not keyed to the temporal, but to the eternal." Rest for him lies in the realm above and beyond material things. If he would lead an unfettered existence, he must throw

away his fetters. We can live with our
aches and pains, but why should the
spirit of man be confined with diseased
organs and aching bones, uttering plain-
tive *ohs* and *ouches* all day long, when it
can, if it will, be free and roam all the
world for sweets.

The desire for rest planted in the heart
of man is no sensual or unworthy one.
It is an evidence of our likeness to God.
It is a proof that we are the children of
God. I believe that it is proof also
that a rest remaineth for the children of
God. But it can and does come to us
only as we become Godlike. If we are
made in God's image, we must share
God's condition,—eternally active, yet
eternally at rest.

"If it be said that man can never attain
this repose because he can never reach the
eternal perfection and power, it may be
answered that it does not depend upon the
proportions of the being, but upon the harmony of his powers, and upon his adjust-
ment to his external condition." If we
could be and keep in perfect harmony with
our environment, we would know rest.

But we cannot have this perfect harmony with our material world. Our bodies are full of animal tendencies and repeatedly and constantly urge us to do things that we will not do. We are at war with our bodies and mean to hold them with firm hands and keep them in subjection so long as we have them. It is good for us, this struggle. It brings pain and suffering and some evil, but it is divinely appointed and has much of blessing and a soul of goodness in it.

But we are more than our bodies, and if we cannot be at peace with them except as we hold them in subjection, let us seek it elsewhere. The butterfly escaping from its chrysalis illustrates our condition. It is dying to its old caterpillar world,—but, oh, how happy it must be rising into its higher life! So it finds rest in becoming. So with you and me. As the real man or woman within, whom the world does not know, but whom we know, swells until it fits its environment and adjusts itself to all that draws it out, then we shall know rest.

"Weariness does not come from action,

but from restraint put upon action." Anything, then, that hinders your growth, prevents your realization of your self, and brings weariness and toil. Unhampered growth into God's image is the rest that remaineth for the children of God. "Man is, properly speaking, based on hope; he has no other possession but hope. This world of his is emphatically the place of hope."

"Rest is not quitting
　　The busy career.
Rest is the fitting
　　Of self to its sphere.

"'Tis the brook's motion,
　　Clear without strife,
Fleeing to ocean
　　After its life.

"'Tis loving and serving
　　The highest and best.
'Tis onward unswerving,—
　　And that is true rest."

IMMORTALITY.

THERE is perhaps no other question in which the world is so deeply interested as in this. The human mind has always held to the belief in immortality, and yet has always doubted it. But the truth of it is not discredited by this fact.

That which can survive so much doubt and so many attacks must have a basis of truth. There is a reason for this struggle, and a reason why we can never be intellectually beyond doubt on this question.

Immortality is a spiritual fact, asserted and demanded by the mind and moral nature of man. Consciousness knows no sleeping or waking. *We* do not sleep. Our bodies cease to bring us reports from the outside world, and yet we know that the real *I* goes on living while it waits for me to waken.

You cannot think of yourself as not

being; you try to identify death and
annihilation, and *you* are standing off at
one side contemplating the ruin you have
wrought. We cannot be conscious of our
minds without being conscious of our independence of time and death. This is
one side of the question. Our bodies
furnish the other. They are constantly
reminding us of death and decay; the
sense of our bodily condition is always
suggesting the impossibility of immortality.

Belief and doubt are the result of an
unending warfare between matter and
spirit. The strength of belief or doubt
in any mind depends entirely upon that
mind's relation to the two domains of
matter and spirit. If matter and its laws
are supreme in the activity of a man, it
will be difficult for him to see any reason
for a belief in immortality. If he lives
in the world-life and knows the spiritual
world, then you cannot convince him of
mortality. Immortality is a fact with him
that needs no proof.

We know that the mind is supreme
over matter, yet this supremacy is limited

by its close subjection to matter. Under
such conditions do we apprehend all high
truths, ethical, mental, and spiritual. No
fact is actually *known* unless it is stated
in mathematical terms, and with questions such as this no demonstration is
possible. It can never become directly
a scientific question, for Science deals
with matter; so, in her attitude toward
this question, she is agnostic. Attempts
to demonstrate this truth degrade it.
Before you can prove it, you must first
bring it down out of the region where
things require no proof to the level of
common things that can be proved. You
may *know* a stone, or a bit of metal,—
you will never weigh love.

Immortality is not proved by Nature.
Nature is full of suggestions and analogies, but analogies prove nothing. Ho-
mologies prove. If we can trace a
homology between any element of our
character and the great nature-world, if
we can find in the great beneficent heart
of God a homology to the heart of man,
we have commenced to build the demonstration of the fact of immortality.

This I wish to do; but first let me refer to some errors in our treatment of the question. Belief in immortality must not be merely a sentiment. By sentiment I mean thought prompted by passion, or desire, or feeling. Primarily, of course, sentiment refers to that state of mind produced by the co-operation of our rational and our moral natures. I refer here to the common indulgence of our emotions, either without a rational basis, or in spite of contradictory rational leadings. When reason fails, we can take refuge in a feeling purely artificial and imaginary. We can produce a feeling of health by the use of stimulants, but it is counterfeit and useless for action. And an artificial feeling of immortality can be produced by the use of stimulants, such as our hymns beginning "There is a happy land, far, far away," or "Sweet fields arrayed in living green," or by the use of what we may call balloon philosophy, which locates both premises and conclusions at such altitudes that the dizzy brain mistakes exaltation for conviction.

In religion we sometimes indulge our sensibilities for the mere excitement of indulgence, allow our imagination to rove for the pleasure of creating scenes of ideal enjoyment and gazing at the airy creation we have made. Here religion has been prostituted, and heavens of sensuality have been interposed between man and the realities of life.

Poetry transformed into a narcotic and emotion produced by a song are often mistaken for the evidence of life. I have already traced the disastrous effects of artificiality of any kind. I think you will require no proof when I say that dreams of Heaven held before a toiling, suffering fellow, do not make toil lighter or suffering less. Do you help a home-sick friend by talking to him of home, or by giving him something else to think about or something to do?

Another mistake is to treat immortality as an abstraction,—as something separated from this life, unconnected with it,—something to be assumed when we get through here. This view of the subject possesses all the evils of sentimentality and one more.   It divides life, subtracts from the energy and interest we should throw into everything we do.   It leads us to temporize; it detracts from the importance of every act, and cultivates low motives, by conditioning our condition hereafter on our behavior here. Immortal life must be very closely identified with this life; life must be immortal, if it is a factor in human development.

So, if I appear to destroy the heaven of your dreams, let me try to show you that in its place may be put a heaven which knows no present or future.

If man is ever to be an immortal being, he is one when he begins to live his divinity.   If you have risen to that height where you feel sure that you know God in this world, and in your life, and in the lives of your fellows, be very sure that you know your own immortality.   For it is life eternal to know God, and his incarnations in Christ and in your brethren. And if you know God now, you know your immortality now.   You know that you are something that cannot die.   How

did Christ view this question? He offers
no proof of immortality, but simply
assumes it. He talks much about love,
faith, obedience, prayer. He might have
shown that each presupposes immortality,
but he did not. Life was so real to him,
that the thought of its ending never seems
to have occurred to him. He was alive,
and that meant alive forever. Death was
only an incident connected with man's
body, and to Christ man was not a body,
but a soul,—using matter for a while,
but not identified with it. If his life
had been to any extent identified with
matter, we might have expected him to
fear death; for we know perfectly that
death will separate us from material
things. But he loved things in men that
death could not touch; he lived and
worked with characters, not bodies. So
death to him was simply a change of
clothes; the life went on. So he wasted
no time in reasoning about things that
are not to be settled by reason. He
assumed God, and God is. To demonstrate immortality would have been to
him irrelevant. He was alive, forever,

self-evident. He assumed it, and built his whole teaching on that assumption.

Do you say that assumption is no proof? It is a statement of conviction. The biologist is convinced that there is such a thing as life; he assumes it, and works upon that assumption. The chemist is convinced that there is such a thing as an atom; he assumes it, and works upon that assumption. So Christ assumes that man is *un*-mortal. He does not speak of life hereafter; life is now— now and forever. Life and eternal life are the same.

This was the reason he talked so much about it. The important thing with him was not that man might through much suffering and trial weather the storms of life, and then have an easy course through all eternity. The vital point with him was, that man should not postpone his good time until after his own funeral, but should begin his eternity now.

So he sought to give meaning to life. Not knowledge, or power, or riches, or position, but character, is what counts.

And when life begins to be true, it
announces itself as eternal to the mind.
"As a caged bird, when let loose into the
sky, might say: 'Now I know that my
wings are made to beat the air in flight;'
and no logic could ever persuade the
bird that it was not designed to fly; but
when caged, it might have doubted, at
times, as it beat the bars of its prison
with unavailing stroke, if its wings were
made for flight." So when a man begins
to live — love, deny himself, serve — he
understands what life is, and knows that
death cannot touch it. But all of these
activities are what may be called spiritual activities. When the spiritual nature
is brought into exercise, it generates not
only faith in eternal life, but reasons
for it.

In proportion as man's life is identified
with things that change and decay is his
faith weakened. But if one's ideals are
in the realm of character, death is not
one of their attributes. Faith has a
wonderful assimilating power; we are
like what we believe. Faith may be
called the workman, our object in life

the pattern, and we are the clay. There is no need that men should be labeled; they confess their faith in feature. By this principle, Christ unites himself to men. Fellowship brings likeness, and likeness means that we take ourselves his attitude toward life. What was his attitude? Love. To the lawyer who tempted him, Christ answered, "Thou shalt love the Lord thy God with all thy heart, and with all thy soul, and with all thy strength, and with all thy mind; and thy neighbor as thyself. This do, and thou shalt live." This is another way of saying life is love, and love is life eternal. Only he who loves lives. Wisdom is vain unless our knowledge is turned into love.

Love for men — and this soon passes into love for God — lifts man above the physical where death is, into the spiritual life everlasting.

RELIGION AS A SOCIAL FACTOR.

THE object of this lecture is to indicate as briefly as the scope of the subject will permit, the part religion may play in the evolution of society. The complex nature of the discussion requires that we should quite clearly understand at the outset the meaning of the terms *religion* and *society*, and something also of the laws that govern the growth of each. Both have suffered because of confusion with other terms, some of which at least have no relation whatever with these whose place they usurp. Many in defining religion will give a definition of ethics or of theology; and the socialist, the communist, and the anarchist each insists on a different definition of society. Let us, then, as carefully as is possible in this limited time, submit each term with its perversions to an analysis that will show us what we mean, and what we do not

mean, by the words *religion* and *society*.
Preliminary to this discussion, however,
it is important to note that both religion
and society have all the characters of living things.   And one peculiarity of living
things is that no concise and inclusive and
limiting definition of them can be written.   Allowance must be made for growth
and change.

If there is ever any place for dogmatiz-
ing, for insisting on final definitions, it is
certainly never found here.   And here,
more than in any other field of knowledge, is one made conscious of mystery.
There is so little, comparatively speaking,
that is founded on fact and experience, that
the temptation to forsake the little that
is known for the much that may be con-
jectured is very strong.   Now the tendency to dogmatize increases as the
subject discussed is lifted out of the
field of experience into that of speculation.   Where nothing can be proved, it
is also true that nothing can be dis-
proved.   Consequently it is true of religion in particular that it carries a great
weight of ghosts and goblins who do

much to hide its real foundation on fact
and experience.   It is still regarded by
many as man's relation to the supernatural.

Every one of the natural sciences to-day
has earned the right to be called *natural*
by long warfare with uncanny dogmas
that usurped the place of law and linked
superstition and religion in a most unholy
struggle to limit the dominion of the
mind.   We have lived to see the angels
chased from astronomy, the devils from
geology, and the ghosts from chemistry.
Judging from the advertising columns of
our papers, physics still has some work
to do with magnetic and electric imps.
But we see mysterious life itself arran-
ging its facts under the domain of law.

In religion alone do angels and ghosts
and devils yet hold their supernatural
sway.   But it is only because in religion
man thinks less than in any other field
of his activity.   Men of apparently strong
common sense will become very freaks in
the name of religion, and act in the house
of worship with a thoughtlessness that
would seem insane in the house of busi-

ness. Not because they are either freaks or fools; they simply prefer not to think,—not to use the same common sense to regulate their relations to their fellow-men and their God that they are quick to use in their business and political relations. From their standpoint, religion is a separate and distinct field of activity. To enter it means that they have by so much widened their responsibility and multiplied their burdens. They prefer to escape both by relegating the whole question to the realm of the supernatural. This shifts responsibility. For common sense knows perfectly that it has no control over the supernatural, and so it gives place to what I would call — if I will not be wrongly interpreted — nonsense. Yet religion, too, will be brought out of the region of the supernatural. No authority on earth can, and no power in Heaven will, withstand man's effort to be a rational being. The more rationally man lives, the more distasteful and useless will the realm of speculation become, and, I hasten to add, the more divine will be the natural.

And Religion will lose nothing by the process. She will gain immensely. Just as we can extend the laws of life into the sphere of religion, just so far will its utility be recognized as a factor in social development. As much as modern chemistry is superior to the useless vagaries of alchemy, will the new religion, now broadening in the world, be superior to the mysticism, the vague emotionalism, the self-deception and spiritual laziness which has too often borne her name.

In prophesying that the future will recognize no other difference between natural and supernatural than between known and unknown, I do not mean that all mystery will vanish. Mystery will never vanish. As the circle of our knowledge widens, the horizon of our world of mystery will widen also. But I do mean that we will cease trying to think of the unknown world except in terms of this world. All that we know of Heaven is here on earth. All that we know of God is in the world of sense and experience. Indeed, we might write a definition of God and say that he is our ideal of goodness and truth and power projected into infinity. When we call him Father, we mean that he is as a perfect father would be; and so with all the attributes we ascribe to him. To be sure, we can and do define him in metaphysical terms, and by so doing make him a metaphysical nonentity, useless in the affairs of men, and affecting them only as a dead weight. If we define our religion as a real social factor, it must be in terms of social life, and God must be recognized as dwelling in men, and not bowed out of his universe before he is made an object of worship.

How pathetic was Christ's attempt to teach his disciples this great truth! Philip, speaking for the twelve, begged him to rend apart the curtains of Heaven and show them the Father; and Jesus says, "Have *I* been so long time with you, and yet hast thou not known me, Philip?"

The only God with whom men can enter into personal relations, then, is to be looked for among men. If he is revealed to men at all, it is in human

terms.   And the religion which is to be
a prominent factor in the regeneration of
society must have a great deal to do with
the affairs of this world, and comparatively little to do with the affairs of
another world.

It requires but a superficial study of
the history of religion to see that one or
the other of the two tendencies referred
to — the tendency toward metaphysics and
the tendency toward submission to authority — has always threatened the usefulness of religion.   There are many
so-called churches to-day that are little
more than philosophical debating socie-
ties or ethical clubs.   The same set of
people, more or less select, will meet
occasionally to consider the affairs of this
world and the next, both at long range,
and narcotize themselves by pleasant intellectual stimulants.   They are as prominent as social factors as would be
articulated skeletons.   And again, there
are churches so dominated by authority
and by dogma that thought is stifled and
society is made like a drove of sheep.
"Whenever metaphysics usurps the place

of religion, the result is spiritual sterility.   When authority takes the place of
reason, the result is intellectual barren-
ness."   Much that passes for religion
to-day is cursed by the metaphysical
formulas of the ancient Greek Church
without the philosophy which gave them
meaning, and by the Latin distrust of
reason without the authority which, while
it enslaved the individual, yet made
dogmatism effective.   Any definition of
religion then must oppose these two
tendencies.

Now, the only remedy for metaphysical
sterility is *life*.   And the only cure for an
intellectually barren slavery to authority
is reason.

Religion then must be defined as both
vital and rational.   Its vitality will be
shown by what it does; its rationality
by its methods and its belief.   Its theology must be tempered by the elasticity
of life.   Theology it must have, as the
body must have a skeleton.   And vitality
it must have, if it is to touch the affairs
of men.

The union of these two elements, vitality and rationality, is possible only when founded on life and experience. Remove religion to a sphere of its own, make it necessary for man to stop doing something else in order to be religious, make it a part of his life, and not all of it, and you devitalize it. It begins to die of heart failure. Lift it above the plane of fact, make faith mean something not in touch with experience, dogmatize when reason fails, and irrational excrescences dignified by metaphysical terms burden the enslaved mind of the superstitious devotee.

We can reason only from the facts and experiences of life — from things which we touch and handle and feel and know. Any system of speculation that starts in the clouds, be it ever so grand, will remain in the clouds and not touch men. And any system of theology to be workable, or any definition of religion that can be lived, must be founded on the experiences of this life, not upon a supposititious life in another realm or hereafter. If the kingdom of Heaven is ever to be realized, it will be as a kingdom on earth; not yonder among the angels and archangels, but here on earth among men and women who, made in God's image, are trying to live like gods.

But let us press closer to our final definition of religion. Religion in the past has been pre-eminently theological. The religion of the present is rapidly becoming a social movement. A definition of religion from the theological side would be "The doing of something by which God, or the superior power, is affected in feeling towards us." God is angry, and must be appeased; we purchase forgiveness by service or sacrifice. Or we need superhuman help; we secure it by certain services which are supposed to be pleasing to Deity.

Now, I am going to deny the adequacy of this definition; but in doing so I must not overlook its element of truth. Sin is a fact of human experience. But all that part of religion which belongs to sacrifice, or the propitiation of the anger of God, belongs to the imagination. It may have been reasoned into a system as elaborate as Calvinism, but it is founded on an imaginary hypothesis. The sacrifice of a beast upon an altar, or of a Son of God upon a cross, for the purpose of averting just retribution from any one, rests upon an imaginary basis which we know is opposed to nature.

Do not misunderstand me. I believe in the atonement. But my conception is far grander than this. Better lift the race above the possibility of sinning than allow it to sin and then lift it above the consequences. Society built upon this hypothesis has always been a society content with its sins. The imagination — even a cultivated one — offers no abiding healthful foundation for practical life; it is an aid to reason, never a safe substitute.

A definition of religion from the standpoint of society would be "Turning from that which is evil to that which is good." It is not a matter of the imagination, but of the heart; not theological or Godward, but sociological or manward. God needs no change — man must change. "Pure religion and undefiled before our God and Father is this, to visit the fatherless and widows in their affliction, and to keep himself unspotted from the world." Religion is *practical love, personal purity*. As a man doeth these things he is religious. This is rational and scientific, practical and vital, and capable of unlimited expansion. . . .

III.— APPENDIX

IN MEMORIAM.

[Professor Murray, in the Stanford *Sequoia*, January 20, 1899.]

DURING this last holiday season the hand of death has been laid upon the sweetest spirit in our midst, and W. W. Thoburn has been taken from us. He died at his home in Palo Alto shortly after eleven o'clock on Friday night, January 6th.

Mr. Thoburn was born June 10, 1859, in Belmont County, Ohio. In 1869 he went to Cincinnati to live, and in 1871 to Washington, D. C. He entered the preparatory department of Columbian University in 1874, and Allegheny College in 1876. In 1881 he graduated with the degree of A. B., and during the succeeding three years held the position of teacher of Natural Science in the Pennsylvania State Normal School. In 1884 he was elected to the chair of Geology and Botany in Illinois Wesleyan University. He pursued a post graduate course of study in biology at Allegheny College, receiving the degrees of A. M. and Ph. D. in 1888.

223

In the same year he was elected to the chair of Geology and Biology in the University of the Pacific, at College Park, Cal., which position he held till the autumn of 1891. He had been received into the California Conference of the Methodist Episcopal Church in 1888, was ordained deacon in 1890, and elder in 1892. After severing his connection with the University of the Pacific in 1891, he was appointed to the pastorate of the Methodist Church in Mayfield.

It was while holding this position that he first came into contact with Stanford University, where he pursued courses of study, even while occupied with the duties of his pastorate. None could have foretold then the place he was to assume among us, but two years later he resigned his charge to accept the position of instructor in zoology and curator of the museum, and definitely took up his work in our University community. From this modest beginning he was advanced until the new department of Bionomics was created and put under his charge. This professorship he held at the time of his death.

He was not yet forty, and he had for years been far from strong; yet it was permitted him to accomplish much,—to make himself

a power. He made those who knew him
love him and love the things he stood for —
earnestness, simplicity, sincerity, and truth;
and those who knew him best loved him
best. In many ways, unique as was his
position, he was representative of the spirit
that obtains among us, and which he loved
to call the Stanford spirit: a spirit of earnestness and of tolerance; a spirit that,
passing over forms, seeks to emphasize the
underlying truth; a spirit that knits together in close union all the various elements of our community. And who shall
say how much of this is due to him?

There were few whom he did not touch,
be it as teacher, as friend, or as spiritual
helper. And yet it would have been a grief
to him to have any one say he was the best-
beloved among us, the one whose influence
was most uplifting. We may say — and to
know that this was our feeling was a joy to
him — that he was one who, in personal
intercourse, in the classroom, and in the
pulpit, made his wide influence tell, not for
scholarship, not for righteousness only, but
for godliness. To measure his work and
his influence is impossible; to number those
in whom he first awakened the desire for
better things; whose eyes he opened to the

noble seriousness of life; those with troubled hearts to whom his own serene and confident faith brought comfort. For the burden of the mystery seemed never to weigh upon his spirit; he was always bright, always cheery, always helpful.

We all looked to him as the one about whom the spiritual life of our community centered. It was easy to talk with him of what lay nearest the heart, or of what weighed heaviest on the heart; it was easy to cherish high ideals, to put away the mean and the low; easy to cling with a vital faith to the divine love whereof he spoke. For some reflection of that love shone in his own face.

Grieve for his loss we must; but as to have known him and loved him has been our privilege, so to carry on his work in measure, by consecrating our own lives to high ends is now our duty. It is thus that he would have us show our love for him and honor his memory.

[President Jordan, at the Memorial Service in the University Chapel, January 29, 1899.]

ONCE when a wise and good man died, these words were said of him: "In whatever part of God's kingdom he may find himself, he will be a hopeful man, looking upward and not downward, looking forward and not backward, ever ready to lend a helping hand, and not afraid to die." In words like these we may express the moving spirit of Thoburn's life. The problems of existence he met simply and seriously, trusting that all truth is God's truth, and all living beings are God's creatures, to be studied and helped, — to be studied in order that they may be wisely helped. To study is the function of science; to help is the mission of religion; and in wisdom and helpfulness lies their true reconciliation.

Thoburn's great intellectual virtue was his open-mindedness. He feared nothing which was true. He cherished nothing which was false. He had learned the difficult lesson that while truth is as broad as the universe, which no mind can span, the line of righteous conduct is as narrow as a footpath compassed by the stride of the child.

In these days knowledge accumulates as never before in all the ages, because men have learned to work together in their search for wisdom. Much that was once wisdom is now superstition. Much that our fathers cherished we cast on the rubbish-heap. Much of the lore of the ancients is but old wives' tales. The narrow creeds which once held religion are too cramped for the new wine of to-day. The life has gone out of the old ceremonies. The old rewards cease to incite to goodness; the old punishments no longer deter from sin. We climb higher each day on the mountain of knowledge, and we look on life in broader and broader perspective. The problem of living truth seems to grow difficult. So many new paths open before us, we know not which it is right to choose, and many have come to doubt whether there be any right path of action.

With all this breadth of knowledge there is no change in man's duty. To do the best he can, moment by moment, day by day, is just as insistent as it ever was. Righteousness is not out of date, nor is piety obsolete. The moral law is just as strenuous to-day as when the stern Hebrew prophets knew of nothing else in the universe. Though creeds lose their validity, and ceremonies fade away, the essence of religion cannot change.

"Still stands thine ancient sacrifice,
A humble and a contrite heart."

The art of receiving new truth with the same simple reverent thankfulness with which he held the oldest truth was one of which Dr. Thoburn was master. He was broad-minded without laxity, tolerant without indifference, free without irreverence. He rejoiced in the winds of freedom, but no part of his religion was blown away by freedom's wayward breezes.

Greater than his intellectual work, greater than his influence as a teacher was the inspiration of his personal life. His own sermons he lived, and this in simple uncon-sciousness, "as the sun gives light, or the flower fragrance." "As the flowers of to-day are the embodiment of past sun-shine," — this was one of his sayings, — "so is the virtue and the happiness of to-day the fruit of the love and altruism of the past." To live again in the virtue and happiness of his students was his greatest ambition as a teacher. And the students knew that they had no wiser adviser, no better friend.

From a letter just received from one of

them, I take these words: "Dr. Thoburn was the religious force of our University. The greatest of all truths was his to show — man's strength in God. Though frail of body, he used faithfully the strength he had, and the little became mighty to serve men. His education was scientific; his experience was deeply human. Because he knew both science and man he could work effectively in an atmosphere of science to reach the heart of men. In our Stanford nook he was our builder, helping us under God's laws to frame solidly housing for ourselves. Science cuts life into facts, and it is our need at Stanford that we should put these together, lest all we take away with us be but a bundle of facts.

"There is danger that Science shall sit in her chair with her cold comment: 'Such is the necessary process of things; let all things take their course.' Love flies to the rescue and stops the bleeding wounds of humanity, by methods Science has revealed. Faith, Hope, and Love drive knowledge into action. To make science a living force for good was Dr. Thoburn's mission. Under such influences Stanford will send out reformers, priests, and poets: zealous men, with warm hearts and trained minds, to save their kind from repeating the sins of yesterday. Souls starving on the dry husks of theology need to be fed with truth fresh seen in the light of this age of science, fresh born from the experience of to-day."

It was Dr. Thoburn's lesson that men should not believe less, but more. Fewer formulated statements, fewer dogmas, it may be, but more deeply, more intensely, more broadly to believe, and to carry all belief over into action.

The place which Dr. Thoburn held in the University was one which made itself. He did not ask to be called as professor of human life, nor did the authorities go out to seek him as such.

He entered the University in 1891 as a graduate student with the rest of the pioneers. When we knew his scholarship we made him assistant in zoology, and from this minor work his own character called him onward. His thoughts and influence were bounded by no chair, and it was not long before his studies broadened to the compass of human life. In a playful way, his colleagues spoke of him as their "spiritual adviser," but behind this jest was perfect seriousness.

He was our spiritual guide, the most

esteemed adviser, the best beloved friend, the one whose loyalty to friendship, whose loyalty to the University, whose loyalty to Christianity, to righteousness and truth, was never questioned. In adding my word to-day, I have not wished to speak of myself, but I cannot refrain from one expression: There is no one who owes Dr. Thoburn a greater debt than I, though I was not the first to realize it or to acknowledge it. In the old garden of the Franciscans, in a far-away city, I received the sad and tender message from Dr. Gilbert: "Our dear friend Thoburn is dead." I was overwhelmed with inexpressible sadness and a feeling almost of discouragement. He was one the University could not spare. All at once the warmth went out from the tropical sunshine. The shadows fell on the white mountain - tops. The delightful tour in the quaint cities around the tall volcanoes, which Dr. Thoburn himself, who knew and loved Mexico, had helped us to plan, seemed to lose its charm. Each of us had lost — from the light of this world — a dear friend. But we all felt more than this. Our beloved University had lost its strongest, its most vital influence for good.

> "The gap in our picked and chosen,
> The long years may not fill."

The place he made is one that must be forever vacant. Other wise and good and Christian men will come and go. Other men will lecture on the unity of life and the soundness of God's universe; but there can be but one Thoburn, and his place in the University must be his alone.

And now we may say again, "In whatever part of God's kingdom he may find himself he will be a hopeful man, looking upward and not downward, looking forward and not backward, ever ready to lend a helping hand, and not afraid to die."

[Dr. Elliott, at the Memorial Service in the University Chapel, January 29, 1899.]

THE first time I ever saw Mr. Thoburn was in the golden summer of 1891. I think he merely passed through my office to talk with President Jordan about the graduate work he hoped to do. He was to be appointed to the pastor's charge at Mayfield, and had as yet no point of contact with the University except the student side of him. And so, when the University opened, he was enrolled in the Department of Zoology. But even at the first he could not remain to us merely a student, and on the twenty-ninth of November, 1891, by invitation of President Jordan, he preached his first sermon in the Chapel — on " Liberty." For two years he maintained the student relation, and then quietly and modestly took his place among us, his life expanding into all the avenues of university activity, his influence widening and deepening as the years went on.

What all this meant to the University in its plastic days we shall realize better by and by. Just now it is the personal side that touches us most keenly; and the inevitable dwelling upon these personal relations is both our pain and our consolation.

His leadership was unmistakable. And yet, it is a word we shall probably use now for the first time. To him the characterization would have seemed absurd; for what he did was without the slightest parade of command. Even in matters where his mastery was undoubted he seemed to trust himself but timidly. Not that he hesitated about doing the thing that needed to be done, but he seemed to depend upon and to need to feel the close-following loyalty of those about him: he could not be quite conscious of the strength and decision which he constantly exhibited. In truth, his leadership was the natural primacy of a full-statured man whose life was rooted in unselfish doing and thinking. He was wise in the deep things of the soul, not by virtue of any subtle philosophy, but through simple, direct living, with open countenance toward the truth wherever he found it. He never met anybody's need by phrases or by subterfuges. He never assumed to solve any problems for you which he had not solved for himself. But he saw into deep depths, and he loved to the uttermost. That he was rewarded by affection, by the trust and confidence of those who doubted and were bewildered, and by a more and more general recognition of the pre-eminence, the simplicity and robustness of his moral leadership, was so natural and spontaneous that we accepted it all without remark and almost without observation.

Some men have religious sides to them. It may be that they are religious intellectually. They absorb and put forth statements about faith, and hope, and love, without ever learning to be really faithful, or hopeful, or loving. Or, they are religious emotionally. Their feelings are touched by religious imagery. They are melted and fused by the simple, universal devotional chords. But when the organ peal has died away, when the rhythmic litany has spent its last beat, they snap back into prosaic sordidness without a trace of the divine brooding which stirred them. If you meet them in the classroom, the laboratory, on the athletic field, or by the fireside, there is no sign of those deeper currents which for the moment seemed the real movement of their lives. It was not so with Mr. Thoburn. He had no religious side. He did not have beliefs or religious emotions which he exercised and cultivated. He was a child of God. His life was of one piece. Its quality was never different, whatever the occasion or situation.

Some men have the gift of tongues. They have a trick of phrasing. We look to them for something impassioned; and in ecclesiastical harness they are brilliant preachers, powerful in prayer, eloquent in testimony. Theirs is the mighty power of swaying human emotions; and yet, what a dangerous gift: for behind it there may be only simulation! He had no such gift. Yet his was a rare power of expression. What he said came straight out of a deep personal experience. Everything had grown in his own garden; and because in his own garden, you knew the flower, you felt the homey fragrance. His experience touched yours in its highest reaches. He phrased out of his own life and aspiration what was active or latent in your life and aspiration. For years, on almost every Sunday, he has spoken the prayer that opens our morning service. How simply and truly he spoke it! It was formal, as all public prayer must be, but it was never made up. It rang true with his own life tones. It reached out for us all and took hold of the hidden springs of life; it touched the heights. And how

in all the little meetings—the morning
Chapel of the old dispensation, the Christian Association of his old, stronger days,
the Vesper Service—he spoke the sure
word, — something searching, something
illuminating, something heartsome!

The twenty-three sermons he preached in
this Chapel were all pre-eminently Stanford
sermons. That is, they met the need, and
traversed the thought, and touched the life
that was developing and ceaselessly flowing
here in our little community. He understood it so well, he believed in it so thoroughly. He revealed us to ourselves. He
brought us to our inheritance. He showed
us the infinite relations. Who that heard
will forget his sermon on "Prayer." Only
a few weeks ago I said to him that he ought
to repeat it every year. But it had met the
need of a particular occasion, and had not
been written down. The words could not be
recalled,—but the fragrance remains. And
his sermon on "The Way," with something
of the deep, fearless, majestic assurance
of the great redwood trees under which
it was written down in those August days
of 1897! And there will always be something unspeakably precious in his last public message, the deep, tender expression, at

Vespers, of the meaning and triumphing
faith of that terrible, newest experience
in his own life when the waters had gone
over his soul.

He spoke once or twice of a volume of
Stanford sermons, a composite of the most
helpful things that had been said in our
Chapel by various men. But for the first
volume of Stanford sermons surely this
only is appropriate: such of his own dis-
courses as by good fortune were committed
to manuscript.

Religion was to him not intellectual formulation of any kind. He did not go about
hewing down barriers which shielded any
other human soul; but for himself he
leaped them all. And he was always dis-
covering to themselves the religious in men.
He worked with many who, having put away
the apparatus of religious expression, had
assumed that they had thereby put aside
their religion. He refused all arbitrary dis-
tinctions. He insisted on counting true men
where they belonged, and sharing to them the
heritage of the Kingdom of God. And so he
was optimistic, hopeful of the religious life
here among us; and the deepening church
and home feeling in our Sunday services,
which he labored so wisely to set growing,

was to him a happy omen of the future activities and associations which should strengthen and hearten the lives of unnumbered generations of students.

The University was also Mr. Thoburn's opportunity. The paths of scholarship opened gratefully to him, and he entered with keen zest upon the fresh ways of original research. Alas, that his zeal so soon outran his strength, and he must pay for his enthusiasm in the familiar way! He never tried to reach so far again, but his work had clearly opened, and for this there had been the long preparation of a life lived out in sincerity and in truth. His own growth was stimulated, and every year we saw his grasp become surer and his horizon wider. How hopefully, even exultingly, his thought leaped to meet the new expansion stirring everywhere in our Stanford air, whose first fruits are the great new buildings already nearing completion or planned for the immediate future! The University made him a part of itself because it could not help it. The University needed — not particularly his scholarship, not particularly the filling of any gaps in its schedule of courses: it needed his manhood, his life-giving quality, his inspiration, his life. It gave his chair differing names: he used to smile at their variety. But there was never any doubt as to the use to be made of him.

And does he cease to be at the University? Is this the end? The time must come when not a student shall know his name. Perhaps some day he will be recalled by none, student or faculty. But the University can never forget his presence. It will never be the same as if he had not lived and worked. Good that is good enough to work in human lives is never 'interred with the bones.'

He lived near to God, and in death he could not be very far from Him. It cannot shake our faith that we shall see his face no more. That he felt, and knew, and cherished the immortal in life is our highest assurance of his immortality. And though we shall see his face no more, there is something that remains. He touched our individual lives. We shall never be quite the same again. We shall have a clearer ideal; we shall have a steadier purpose; we shall face life with greater courage.

The work he did here, the work he left undone, this he would not have chosen that we remember. Hallam Tennyson tells of his father's last visit to Frederick Tennyson,

in the Isle of Wight. "When the brothers
bade 'good-bye' they thought that they
would not in this life see each other again:
'Good-night, true brother, here, good-morrow
there.'" So he would have parted with us,
and so he would wish to be remembered:
just in the spirit of comradeship, and in the
bonds of good-fellowship. A brave fare-
well, and facing the future!

NOT by his simple eloquence he won,
Straightforward as the story of a child;
Not by his doctrines, pure and undefiled,
Drawn from the teachings of his Father's
 Son;

Not by his deep devotion to the truth —
Fearless he faced it, piercing every cloud,
He spurned the trammels by the Church
 allowed —
He homage drew from child, age, manhood,
 youth.

But this: that never word or act of sham
Was his; he could have taught us: "As I am,
Be all of you;" his eloquence he lived;
The truth he sought and found, and loved, he
 lived;
Between his doctrines and himself no strife:
He lived them.   And men loved him for his
 life.

JOSEPH HUTCHINSON.

January 15, 1899.